SEIZING TRIUMPH
FROM TRIALS

Learning How to Overcome Trials

Rick Carter Jr. Ph.D.

Seizing Triumph from Trials
Copyright © 2021 by Rick Carter Jr. Ph.D. All rights reserved.

No part of this publication may be reproduced, stored in a retrieval system or transmitted in any way by any means, electronic, mechanical, photocopy, recording or otherwise without the prior permission of the author except as provided by USA copyright law.

The opinions expressed by the author are not necessarily those of URLink Print and Media.

1603 Capitol Ave., Suite 310 Cheyenne, Wyoming USA 82001
1-888-980-6523 | admin@urlinkpublishing.com

URLink Print and Media is committed to excellence in the publishing industry.

Book design copyright © 2021 by URLink Print and Media. All rights reserved.

Published in the United States of America

Library of Congress Control Number: 2021904106
ISBN 978-1-64753-711-1 (Paperback)
ISBN 978-1-64753-712-8 (Digital)

09.12.20

CONTENTS

Acknowledgments v
Introduction vii

How Not to Deal with Trials 1
The Lord Sees You 10
Do You Believe in God through the Trial? 18
Put the Past Behind You 27
Walk with God 37
Be Diligent in the Business That God Gives You to Do 51
Resist Temptation 60
Be a Servant 69
Learn Patience 77
Whose Fault Is It That You're Sad? 91
Here We Test Again 100
God Brought Me Here 110
How to Get the Blessing After the Trial 120
Different Ways to Deal with Trials 129
Things You Need to Know to Make It through Life 140

ACKNOWLEDGMENTS

I would like to thank all those who have made this work possible. There are so many who have contributed to my personal spiritual growth over the years that trying to single out each and every one would be an impossibility; but the following people have had such a significant impact on my life that I cannot neglect to acknowledge them.

Thank you to Rick and Eunice Carter, my parents, who taught their children that life is an adventure and serving the Lord is a great reward. I appreciate your example of faith and steady determination to following God's will in life no matter the circumstances or trials that you faced.

Thank you to Angela Carter, my wife who, through good times and bad, has been my greatest supporter and whose presence always causes me to desire to draw nearer to my Lord. I am so thankful for your love and desire to follow the leadership of God in our lives as my wife and the mother of our children.

Thank you to Dr. Ivan Casteel and Dr. Mike Hays, my pastor and my teacher. The lessons that God used you to teach me are a large part of the reason that I am serving God as I am today. Thank you for your godly examples and firm stand on the truth of God's Word.

Finally, I would like to thank Beth Haven Baptist Church, my family. It is such a great honor to be your pastor and to watch you grow in Christ. I have told you many times that life isn't about what happens to you, it is about how you respond to it. I have seen you respond to both blessings and trials and watched God's grace shine as you have humbled to Him through them all. I appreciate your partnership as we serve God together and your support as we have the opportunity to reach beyond the doors of our church building to help the hurting in our world. I pray for God's richest blessings on you as we continue to walk together in His light.

INTRODUCTION

Nothing that draws you closer to God is a bad thing. That is a hard statement, but a truth that each person must grab hold of if they are going to seize triumph from the tragedies of their life. God never hid the fact that we would face trials in our life. He had Job record in Job 5:7: "Yet man is born unto trouble, as the sparks fly upward." And in Job 14:1 "Man *that is* born of a woman *is* of few days, and full of trouble." Truer words were never spoken. The making of life is not about what happens to us, rather, it is about how we respond. The same event can happen to two people and produce in one anger bitterness and defeat, but in the other humility, purpose, and joy. The difference is not the event but the attitude that it meets in us.

One of the greatest paradoxes in the Bible is the command found in 1 Thessalonians 5:18 "In every thing give thanks: for this is the will of God in Christ Jesus concerning you." How can we in fact give thanks for the bad things that happen in our lives? How can we give thanks when trials knock us down? I would submit to you that those are the exact times that God is speaking of giving thanks in. When we learn the secret of praising God, not just *in* the trials, but *for* the trials, we have crossed over into a victorious Christian living that few attain. That crossing comes when we accept the truth that nothing that draws us closer to God is a bad thing. This is how we can thank God for trials and thank God for enemies that rise up against us.

I am convinced that peace, joy, and meaning in life are the result of the trials that we face rather than the calm that we desire. God's own example on the cross demonstrates for us that He never intended to prevent suffering in our lives but rather He has chosen to overcome it. He said in Ephesians 5:1–2: "Be ye therefore followers of God, as dear children; And walk in love, as Christ also hath loved us, and hath given himself for us an offering and a sacrifice to God for a sweetsmelling savour." The example that we have of what makes life sweet is the life of trial and sacrifice that our Saviour led. The Bible says in Hebrews 12:2: "Looking unto Jesus the author and finisher of *our* faith; who for the joy that was set before him endured the cross, despising the shame, and is set down at the right hand of the throne of God." The idea that trials and suffering could ever be counted as joy is contrary to our natural thinking, but it is directly in line with God's divine thinking.

It is my earnest desire that through the reading of this book you will receive the assistance of the Holy Spirit of God to face the trials of your life with a new view and live in the joy of God regardless of the circumstances of life that you are facing. Embrace the trials that you have rather than fighting against them and use them to draw you closer to the Lord Jesus Christ. For nothing that helps us to do that could ever be a bad thing in our lives.

HOW NOT TO DEAL WITH TRIALS

And there was a famine in the land: and Abram went down into Egypt to sojourn there; for the famine *was* grievous in the land. And it came to pass, when he was come near to enter into Egypt, that he said unto Sarai his wife, Behold now, I know that thou *art* a fair woman to look upon: Therefore it shall come to pass, when the Egyptians shall see thee, that they shall say, This *is* his wife: and they will kill me, but they will save thee alive. Say, I pray thee, thou *art* my sister: that it may be well with me for thy sake; and my soul shall live because of thee. And it came to pass, that, when Abram was come into Egypt, the Egyptians beheld the woman that she *was* very fair. The princes also of Pharaoh saw her, and commended her before Pharaoh: and the woman was taken into Pharaoh's house. And he entreated Abram well for her sake: and he had sheep, and oxen, and he asses, and menservants, and maidservants, and she asses, and camels. And the LORD plagued Pharaoh and his house with great plagues because of Sarai Abram's wife. And Pharaoh called Abram, and said, What *is* this *that* thou hast done unto me? why didst thou not tell me that she *was* thy wife? Why saidst thou, She *is* my sister? so I might have taken her to me to wife: now therefore behold thy wife, take *her*, and go thy

1

way. And Pharaoh commanded *his* men concerning him: and they sent him away, and his wife, and all that he had.

Genesis 12:10–20

Famine is defined by the Webster's 1828 dictionary first as "the scarcity of food, dearth, and a general want of provisions sufficient for the inhabitants of a place." The second definition that they list is, "want, destitution, such as a famine of the word of life."

We are familiar with the concept of famine, but to the best of my searching, I was unable to find any record of a famine in the US other than the 1930s depression. However, during that time, in order to undergird the business, the government categorized any food that the stores couldn't sell as redundant and destroyed them by burning crops in the field, dumped them in the ocean, and plowed under ten million hectares of harvesting fields as well as killing 6.5 million pigs according to one source that I read.

Throughout history, however, famines have been a source of fear and pain to many nations. The majority of times that I read about famines in other lands, the end result was anywhere from a quarter to half of the population dying. There is no doubt that the prospects of starving to death would have motivated Abraham to seek out some other options, though his overall response, as we will see, was not a proper response.

Before we get into the specifics of Abraham's response to this adversity, consider with me what the Bible says about famine. We are told that God calls for famine at times as He did in 2 Kings 8:1: "Then spake Elisha unto the woman, whose son he had restored to life, saying, Arise, and go thou and thine household, and sojourn wheresoever thou canst sojourn: for the LORD hath called for a famine; and it shall also come upon the land seven years." In this passage, famine was brought by God for the purpose of judgment. However, not all famines were for the purpose of judgment. It would appear that the famines that occurred during the lives of Abraham, Isaac, and Jacob were for the purpose of testing in the lives of these men. At times, God allows trials to come into our lives that there seems to be no earthly answer for. There was no one who could help and there were limited options to choose from. Too often we run from trials by taking the easy way out. This type of trial, however, provided no such option.

God didn't leave us without instruction on how to handle such situations in life. However, He has given His children instructions of what to do during a time of famine. In 1 Kings 8:35–40, God said: "When heaven is shut up, and there is no rain, because they have sinned against thee; if they pray toward this place, and confess thy name, and turn from their sin, when thou afflictest them: Then hear thou in heaven, and forgive the sin of thy servants, and of thy people Israel, that thou teach them the good way wherein they should walk, and give rain upon thy land, which thou hast given to thy people for an inheritance. If there be in the land famine, if there be pestilence, blasting, mildew, locust, or if there be caterpiller; if their enemy besiege them in the land of their cities; whatsoever plague, whatsoever sickness there be; What prayer and supplication soever be made by any man, or by all thy people Israel, which shall know every man the plague of his own heart, and spread forth his hands toward this house: Then hear thou in heaven thy dwelling place, and forgive, and do, and give to every man according to his ways, whose heart thou knowest; (for thou, even thou only, knowest the hearts of all the children of men;) That they may fear thee all the days that they live in the land which thou gavest unto our fathers."

God also said in 2 Chronicles 20:9, "If, when evil cometh upon us, as the sword, judgment, or pestilence, or famine, we stand before this house, and in thy presence, (for thy name is in this house,) and cry unto thee in our affliction, then thou wilt hear and help."

So the Biblical answer to adversity, such as famine, is to first confirm your proper relationship with the Lord, secondly confess any sin and forsake it, and finally to pray and seek the presence of God. These three steps are necessary parts of the everyday life of the believer as well. We must keep a clear account with God and maintain a fervent relationship.

Will this cause the famine to stop? Not necessarily, but it will accomplish the following things: First, the Bible tells us that God will redeem you. In Job 5:17–20, the Bible says, "Behold, happy is the man whom God correcteth: therefore despise not thou the chastening of the Almighty: For he maketh sore, and bindeth up: he woundeth, and his hands make whole. He shall deliver thee in six troubles: yea, in seven there shall no evil touch thee. In famine he shall redeem thee from death: and in war from the power of the sword."

The scriptures also declare that God will keep you during times of famine if your trust is in Him in Psalms 33:18–19: "Behold, the eye of the LORD is upon them that fear him, upon them that hope in his mercy; To deliver their soul from death, and to keep them alive in famine."

The Lord goes on to say that He will provide for you in Psalms 37:18–19: "The LORD knoweth the days of the upright: and their inheritance shall be for ever. They shall not be ashamed in the evil time: and in the days of famine they shall be satisfied."

The problem is that we don't often respond to times of extreme trial in our lives in this manner. We often respond in the wrong way during these times. God knew that we would, so he allowed us to see the results of responding wrong in the Scriptures. As a matter of fact, Abraham responded wrong as well. We have the benefit of being able to look back on these events, remember that Abraham didn't have the same luxury. He also didn't have two other important things that we have: the complete Word of God and the indwelling of the Holy Spirit. Even with these three great gifts, we often respond wrongly just as Abraham did. For that reason, I want you to take note of the response that He had.

He left the presence of God's promise. As we have just read, Abraham had just received the greatest promise ever given to a nation. He had just built two altars to the Lord. The second of which he called Bethel or the house of God. Yet, immediately after this mountaintop spiritual experience, he allows the fear of famine to drive him out of the inheritance.

I would like to think that my faith would be strong enough to stay if I had just received such a promise, but I fear that I am just as human as Abraham. Instead of responding in the power of the promise of God, Abraham responded in the fear of the flesh. This fear grips the heart and mind of many, the fear that there will not be provision enough where God has called them. If I surrender to that call, how will my family be fed? How will my house be provided for? How will we take care of our medical needs? How will we…?

God, I know you just called me here, and you have given me a great promise, and I will gladly stay and obey you as soon as there are no difficulties that I see. As soon as there is no trial, I will go, Lord. As soon as my bills are all paid and my 401K is fully funded and my stock portfolio is recovered and I have all the things that I want, I will go, I will tithe, I will serve, I will…You see, God allowed this adversity to come in Abraham's life to test his faith, for God to provide where He had called, and Abraham failed the test when he departed from the place of promise.

How often have you or I failed such a test? I find that often after I have surrendered to follow the Lord's direction in my life, I am immediately plunged into a trial of my faith. I believe that at times, God does this to test the sincerity of our commitment to trust and follow Him. Will this little adversity stop them?

As I consider this, I am reminded of the disciples as they had just seen Jesus perform the great miracle of feeding the five thousand. Jesus put them into the boat and commanded them to go to the other side while he went up to pray. There they were in the absolute will of God, they couldn't have nailed the will of God for that moment any better. God Himself in the form of Jesus Christ had personally shown them where to go and had audibly told them what to do. Yet, there in the absolute center of God's will, the first thing that happens is adversity; the storm arises, the winds blow, and the sea is boisterous. And do they seek God in prayer? Do they have faith that God is going to accomplish the task that He has sent us on? No, they cry out in fear.

You see, God has to put us in the place where we realize that this task that He has given us, this calling that He has made, is not to be accomplished by our power; it is not by our might, it is by His Spirit that the work will be done. So He reminds us of that through adversity when we have surrendered to His call.

Remember, He brings these times upon us, nothing happens outside of His will; He wants us to pray, He wants us to seek His face, He wants us to depend upon Him, but what we often do is just what

Abraham did—we run. We say, "Okay, God, you must not have been ready yet. I will be back later when you are more prepared." But friend, if that is our response, we have missed the big picture of how God wants to work in our lives.

He went after the provision of the world. Not only did Abraham leave from the place of promise, but he also went down to Egypt, which is always a picture of the world. He didn't just go to another part of the promised land, which was vast; he decided to get completely out of the promise and go down to Egypt. There is no telling how many people, who have been called to the promises of God, are sitting in a spiritual Egypt right now.

Many are seeking the provision of the world rather than experiencing the provision of God. After leaving Egypt, Israel often lusted after the leeks and the garlics that the world had to offer, rather than basking in the wonder of the provision of faith. I tell you, I have seen both and I would choose the blessing of seeing the hand of God providing any day over the provision of the world.

It is exciting to watch God do what this world thinks is impossible. If you have been called to walk by faith, don't stoop to live in the mansions of this world.

Several years ago, my assistant pastor and I sat in the office of a vice-president of a large school and shared with him the vision that God has given us here at Beth Haven to have a school that is funded by faith, no tuition. He informed us that he didn't think that it would work. I said, praise the Lord, it isn't about what people think when it comes to the will of God; it is about what God thinks. God provides where he calls, and the techniques, plans, and philosophies of this world are often the things that keep us from reaching the height of joy that comes through a life surrendered by faith.

I am not saying that it is sin for a Bible college to charge tuition, but I am saying that if God has said for them not to, they had better trust in the foolishness of faith, rather than the business plan of the world. And that goes for any area of life. Stay out of the world's provision, keep yourself in the place where you need to be, and long for the provision from on high.

The reason that most don't hunger and thirst after the blessings of God is that they are so full of the provision of this world. They think that they are rich and increased with goods and have need of nothing and that they do not know that they are wretched and miserable and poor and blind and naked.

The worst part of that was that Abraham taught his family that the world was an acceptable option to the trials of God, and they continually sought to evade trials by fleeing to Egypt. Rebellious children sought the counsel of the world over the counsel of God, the covering and protection of this world over the protection of God. Isaiah 30:1 says, "Woe to the rebellious children, saith the LORD, that take counsel, but not of me; and that cover with a covering, but not of my spirit, that they may add sin to sin."

Abraham denied the promise of faith. He denied the promise of faith by leaving the land of promise, he denied the promise of faith by seeking the provision of the world, and denied the promise of faith by lying about his wife. For Abraham, this was a half-lie, Sarah was his half-sister, but a half-truth is a whole lie.

Abraham's children learned this lesson as well. Isaac tried the same thing when he fled down to Egypt and lied about his wife, and Jacob was just named deceiver. Your failure to follow the plan of God in your life doesn't affect only you but it also affects your whole family. It almost cost Sarah her purity; it almost cost Abraham his wife.

I can't imagine that it played out well for him for the rest of his life as every time they had a fight Sarah could always pull out, "Well, I never asked you to tell anyone you were my brother instead of my husband." Once you start running from God, there is no limit to the sin you will find yourself in. I don't imagine that Abraham would have ever desired to put his wife in danger, or deny her, but that is what happens when you are running from the testing of God. Sin will take you farther than you want to go, keep you longer than you want to say, and cost you far more than you want to pay.

Sin always destroys everything it touches. Your compromises today will lead you to your sins tomorrow. We live in a day of famine, not of food right now, but as it says in Amos 8:11, "Behold, the days come, saith the Lord GOD, that I will send a famine in the land, not a famine of bread, nor a thirst for water, but of hearing the words of the LORD."

We live in a day when God has called His children to live in the promises of His Word and has placed a calling to reach the world with the Gospel on every one of us. He has maybe called some to full-time service, and there is in our day a famine of hearing the words of the Lord. If you submit to the call, there will be trials. There is no easy place of service, but God has called and He will sustain. God has never forsaken His children. If you have recently surrendered to the call of God in your life—whatever it is, from church membership to missionary service—you can expect that there will be adversities that would come. Don't respond in the flesh, but respond by faith instead.

THE LORD SEES YOU

And he went in unto Hagar, and she conceived: and when she saw that she had conceived, her mistress was despised in her eyes. And Sarai said unto Abram, My wrong *be* upon thee: I have given my maid into thy bosom; and when she saw that she had conceived, I was despised in her eyes: the LORD judge between me and thee. But Abram said unto Sarai, Behold, thy maid *is* in thy hand; do to her as it pleaseth thee. And when Sarai dealt hardly with her, she fled from her face. And the angel of the LORD found her by a fountain of water in the wilderness, by the fountain in the way to Shur. And he said, Hagar, Sarai's maid, whence camest thou? and whither wilt thou go? And she said, I flee from the face of my mistress Sarai. And the angel of the LORD said unto her, Return to thy mistress, and submit thyself under her hands. And the angel of the LORD said unto her, I will multiply thy seed exceedingly, that it shall not be numbered for multitude. And the angel of the LORD said unto her, Behold, thou *art* with child, and shalt bear a son, and shalt call his name Ishmael; because the LORD hath heard thy affliction. And he will be a wild man; his hand *will be* against every man, and every man's hand against him; and he shall dwell in the presence of all his brethren. And she called the name of the LORD that spake unto her, Thou God seest me: for she said, Have I also here looked after him that seeth me? Wherefore the well was called Beerlahairoi; behold, *it is* between Kadesh and Bered. And Hagar bare Abram a son: and Abram called his son's name, which Hagar bare, Ishmael. And Abram *was* fourscore and six years old, when Hagar bare Ishmael to Abram.

Genesis 16:4–16

The Scriptures tell us here that once Hagar realized that she was pregnant, she despised Sarai. Sarai realized the error of her idea and promptly blamed Abram, who did what any husband would do and said, "Do whatever you want to, dear." So Sarai, the Bible says, dealt hardly with her, which is an ambiguous statement at best because it could mean anything from giving her harder work to do to giving her the whip as a servant. Either way, Hagar was so disposed because of the action to flee from her mistress.

This passage is the first time we read of Hagar, but we know according to the text that she was an Egyptian. It is fit then to think that she may have been acquired when Abram and Sarai were residing there a few chapters back. The Bible tells us that as she ran away, she was headed to Shur. We are told in 1 Samuel 15:7: "And Saul smote the Amalekites from Havilah until thou comest to Shur, that is over against Egypt." So Hagar was not only running away, she was running back to her old life.

Listen, friend, there are always going to be struggles and conflicts in life, but the old flesh always wants to convince us to run back to the world when they arise. The natural response of the flesh is to go back to our old sinful nature and the sins we found as comfortable in the past. One of the best ways that you can know if you are walking in the Spirit is in how you respond when you have conflict arising. Do you fall to your knees? Do you immerse yourself in the Word and in prayer? Or do you resort to your old besetting sins? When conflict triggers your response, what is it?

Hagar is a picture of the flesh fleeing in the face of trials and was heading back to the old life. Notice the wording in verse 7: she was 'by the fountain in the way to Shur." I know that most of the time, we would overlook this as just a grammatical thing, but I don't believe God wastes words. God put that fountain in the way to cause her to stop. She was running through a wilderness, through a desert, and in the way was a fountain of water; of course, she was going to stop. Praise God when God puts something in our way when we are running away from His will.

I wonder how many times we have been fleeing, in a panicked flight of the flesh, when God put a well in our way to stop us so that He could speak to us and counsel us. But we passed right by and didn't listen to Him until it was too late and the consequences of our sin became greater than we imagined they could be.

I want you to take note that the Bible says that she was found by the angel of the LORD. When the word LORD is in all capitals in the Old Testament, it indicates that it is speaking of Jehovah. However, this is the first time that the phrase the angel of the LORD is used in the Old Testament, and when it is used it is generally considered to be a Christophany or a representation of the Lord Jesus Christ. Later in verse 13, she calls the angel of the LORD simply LORD and then identifies Him as God Himself, calling Him both Jehovah and El, the Hebrew word for God.

Now for the purpose of our study here, I want us to focus in on verse 8, because here the LORD engages in one of the first counseling sessions that I have seen in the Bible. Remember, Isaiah 9:6 tells us, "For unto us a child is born, unto us a son is given: and the government shall be upon his shoulder: and his name shall be called Wonderful, Counsellor, The mighty God, The everlasting Father, The Prince of Peace."

In our counseling seminary, we emphasize that there is only one counselor, and that is the LORD Jesus Christ. He is the great counselor, and we are only tools that He uses to guide people to His counsel. I have nothing to give you of myself, no other counselor has anything to give you of themselves if they are honest. The only thing that we have to offer is direction to the counsel of the wonderful counselor, the LORD Jesus Christ.

I want you to take special care of this to notice how He counsels her then, because if we will seek Him, He will counsel us through the trials that we face each and every day.

This divine counseling session with the Lord begins by asking two questions:

1. Whence camest thou? Or, where did you come from? What has happened to you? Often I will begin a counseling session with, "Tell me why you are here."
2. The second question is whither wilt thou go? Or, where are you headed?

Now these two questions are vital to resolving the issues that people come into counseling for. What happened, and what are you doing about it?

I want you to notice here that she only answered the first question. She responded, "I flee from the face of my mistress Sarai." She didn't answer the second question, she didn't want to acknowledge that she was running back to Egypt. It is rare to counsel someone who says I intend to ruin my life because of what has happened. But that is where they are headed, though often they will not admit it.

Hagar was put into this situation; she was serving faithfully and was told, "Now you are going to be Abram's wife." She obeyed, and up to that point, she hadn't done wrong in the situation. Her problem was not that she did something wrong; it was how she responded after others made bad decisions—she despised Sarai. I tell my church often that life is not about what happens to you, life is about how you respond to it. So Hagar first responded wrong to Sarai by despising her, and then she responded wrong by running away. One bad decision usually leads to another.

The problem is that most of us are so prideful that we will not go back and face the music for our bad decisions; rather, we just run and keep on running. I fear that churches are full today of people who have responded the wrong way to conflict in one place. Only to run and find another place but never fix the problem that started the whole thing. So they take the wrong spirit from one situation to another, and from one church to another and before long, they set a habit of church hopping every time something happens again and they never resolve anything.

Yes, sometimes God moves people, but I don't believe God moves people as often as some people do. I think more often it is because we have gotten our feelings hurt and we have been unwilling to humble ourselves to right the situation, and it is easier to run. Hagar sure thought so, and so does everyone who is operating in the flesh.

So the LORD gives Hagar the counsel she desperately needed but most likely didn't want, and it was twofold.

1. Return—Go back to where the problem began and face the issue.
2. Submit—Humble yourself to the situation and the people that you are running from.

I want you to understand that until you go back and face the problem, you will never resolve it. You will always be running, you will always be in conflict no matter how long it is, and no matter how far you run, you cannot run away from your own conscience. Some try to run into a bottle, some into drugs, or any other form of worldliness, but it doesn't take away the pain of the conflict, it only magnifies the sorrow.

Here is the truth, in verse ten, God begins to reveal what Hagar couldn't see and that is what He wanted to accomplish in her life because of this trial. Our vision is finite, we cannot see what God has in store for our lives. All she could see was the hardship of this current trial. She couldn't see the things that God had planned for her and her child. God shared with her some of the things that He had in store here.

Friend, often we run when trials come along, and we are fleeing from the very thing that God wanted to use to give us our greatest blessing.

You and I rebel against God because we think that we know what is best; we think that we should never have a trial, we should never have a conflict, and that if we do, it must mean that God isn't watching out for us. But the exact opposite is true. It was indeed God who took her through the trial, and it is God who wants to take you through your trails. If you will trust Him and depend upon Him, He will guide you safely through.

Quit trying to fix what God is doing in your life. Just return and submit to what He has planned. If we could get that down, it would eliminate the majority of our counseling. If we would just keep our eyes on Jesus and trust Him through our trials, instead of rebelling and running, we wouldn't have the emotional problems that we create for ourselves.

I am telling you that we need to come to the same place that Hagar did in verse 13 when she says, "Thou God seest me." When we come to the place that we acknowledge that God sees us in the midst of our trials, in the midst of our conflict when we think that He has forsaken us, when we cannot possibly see what or how God could use such a horrible event, when we do not understand, He still sees us.

It is possible, as we said, that Hagar was beaten. But how could God have allowed that? God saw the big picture. He saw what the ultimate outcome would be, and, though we cannot understand the minute twists and turns of life, He sees it all. Though we cannot understand the why, He knows the end goal and it is not up to us to sit around and figure it all out. Figuring it all out will not bring you peace; returning and submitting will.

Wait a minute, submitting to the one that caused our problem? No, submitting to God. They are only the physical tool that God is using to teach us submission, just as Jesus learned submission in the same way. Hebrews 5:8 says, "Though he were a Son, yet learned he obedience by the things which he suffered."

Let me preface here that I am not condoning abuse, and I am not saying that someone should put themselves in a situation where they might be abused. I am speaking of dealing with trials in general. In such situations that a person has done physical abuse, the authorities should be involved, and until there is confidence that there is no physical harm that it will happen again, they should not return. The Bible clearly says in Proverbs 22:24, "Make no friendship with an angry man; and with a furious man thou shalt not go."

In reference, however, to trials in general, once you learn first to submit yourself to God in those trials, the physical proximity to those who caused them will not be a problem. Once you remember that He is the Soverign ruler of the universe and all power and authority comes from Him, it will not be a problem to submit yourself to earthly authorities.

In our text, we find that Hagar did return and bore a son, and Abraham named him Ishmael, which means "God will hear."

Friend, remember, God sees you and God hears you and God has a plan for your life. Your submission to the trials of your life is key to reaching the finish line. Resist walking in the flesh when you are tried; rather, say as Job did in Job 23:10: "But he knoweth the way that I take: when he hath tried me, I shall come forth as gold."

DO YOU BELIEVE IN GOD THROUGH THE TRIAL?

And it came to pass after these things, that God did tempt Abraham, and said unto him, Abraham: and he said, Behold, *here* I *am*. And he said, Take now thy son, thine only *son* Isaac, whom thou lovest, and get thee into the land of Moriah; and offer him there for a burnt offering upon one of the mountains which I will tell thee of. And Abraham rose up early in the morning, and saddled his ass, and took two of his young men with him, and Isaac his son, and clave the wood for the burnt offering, and rose up, and went unto the place of which God had told him. Then on the third day Abraham lifted up his eyes, and saw the place afar off. And Abraham said unto his young men, Abide ye here with the ass; and I and the lad will go yonder and worship, and come again to you. And Abraham took the wood of the burnt offering, and laid *it* upon Isaac his son; and he took the fire in his hand, and a knife; and they went both of them together. And Isaac spake unto Abraham his father, and said, My father: and he said, Here *am* I, my son. And he said, Behold the fire and the wood: but where *is* the lamb for a burnt offering? And Abraham said, My son, God will provide himself a lamb for a burnt offering: so they went both of them together. And they came to the place which God had told him of; and Abraham built an altar there, and laid the wood in order, and bound Isaac his son, and laid him on the altar upon the wood. And Abraham stretched forth his hand, and took the knife to slay his son. And the angel of the LORD called unto him out of heaven, and said, Abraham, Abraham: and he said, Here *am* I. 12 And he said, Lay not thine hand upon the lad, neither do thou any thing unto him: for now I know that thou fearest God, seeing thou hast not withheld thy son, thine only *son* from me. And Abraham lifted up his eyes, and looked, and behold behind *him* a ram caught in a thicket by his horns: and Abraham went and took the ram, and offered him up for a burnt offering in the stead of his son. And Abraham called the name of that place Jehovahjireh: as it is said *to* this day, In the mount of the LORD it shall be seen. And the angel of the LORD called unto Abraham out of heaven the second time, And said, By myself have I sworn, saith the LORD, for because thou hast done this thing, and hast not withheld thy son, thine only *son*: That in blessing I will bless thee, and in multiplying I will multiply thy seed as the stars of the heaven, and as the sand which *is* upon the sea shore; and thy seed shall possess the gate of his enemies; And in thy seed shall all the nations of the earth be blessed; because thou hast obeyed my voice. So Abraham returned unto his young men, and they rose up and went together to Beersheba; and Abraham dwelt at Beersheba.

Genesis 22:1–19

This is a rich passage in spiritual truth and beautiful pictures of our Lord Jesus Christ. I want to take a few minutes to make a few observations before we get into the heart of the text.

There are two things that are mentioned here for the first time. The first is in verse one, this is the first time that we find the idea of God proving to anyone. It says in verse one that God did tempt Abraham. Now we know that God does not tempt men to do evil, it tells us in James 1:13: "Let no man say when he is tempted, I am tempted of God: for God cannot be tempted with evil, neither tempteth he any man." The word *tempt* here in Genesis is not speaking of temptation to evil but is interchangeable with the word *prove*. The same word is translated *tempt* or *prove* alternately in many places such as in Exodus 20:20, which says, "And Moses said unto the people, Fear not: for God is come to prove you, and that his fear may be before your faces, that ye sin not."

So the Lord had no intention of allowing Abraham to sacrifice Isaac on that day, but He wanted to prove to him, to test him, to know the sincerity of his heart. This is the first time that we find the Lord testing anyone in the Bible. We will speak more of this in a few minutes.

The second first that we see here is in verse two. This is the first time in the Bible that we see the word *love*. It is interesting to note that it is in reference to the love of a father for His son. What makes it even more interesting is that the first time we see the word *love* in the New Testament is when Jesus was baptized and God the Father spoke from heaven and said, "This is My beloved Son, in whom I am well pleased." So the first time we see the word *love* in the New Testament is an expression of love from the Heavenly Father to the Son. What a glorious picture of God's great love that we are beholding here in Genesis.

Now the combination of these two things leads us to the thought that we are going to examine. There are times of testing for everyone who is a believer. There are times that God asks us for things in our lives that are beyond our comprehension. I cannot imagine what it must have been like for Abraham the day that God told him to take his son and offer him for a burnt offering. I have great love for my children. I love my girls and my boys, and I cannot imagine what it would be like for me if God spoke to me and said, "Take your son and offer him as a burnt offering."

One might respond with, "I don't know what you are asking. How could you ask for that?" And let me say that this is an extreme example, but there is a principle that is present here that everyone of us need to get. It is the principle that is found in the first and greatest commandment. In Matthew 22:37–38, it tells us, "Jesus said unto him, Thou shalt love the Lord thy God with all thy heart, and with all thy soul, and with all thy mind. This is the first and great commandment."

We need to understand that God has the right to ask for anything. He has the right to take anything. He is God! But we get the idea that there are some things that are off-limits to God. We say things like, "Lord, I want you to be in control of my life, as long as you don't go to far. As long as you don't ask for my children, as long as you don't ask for my money, as long as you don't ask for my time, or my life. Other than those things, You have complete control." Really? That isn't the kind of complete control that God is looking for.

Let's be honest, most of us would have failed the test that was given to Abraham that day. Most of us would have balked at the command of God. As a matter of fact, many, if not most of us, have denied lesser requests from God in our lives. When God has asked us for something in our lives to be given to Him and we have said no, we have foolishly and wrongly held onto those things that He has asked us for.

I suppose that Abraham could have said, "This isn't fair, God. I have just received him. After all the years of waiting on you to fulfill the promise of a son, how could you ask for him back? What about the promise of children from him? How could you break that promise?" He could have begun to argue with God, he could have begun to be angry with God, what kind of a God would ask for such a thing? He could have been in denial, that this wasn't really God speaking to him, and thus, he didn't have to obey. There are a myriad of things that could have gone through Abraham's mind, but only one thing did.

What was that one thing that went through his mind? "I love God more than anything else in this world. I believe that He will do what He has said he would do, He can be trusted and He knows what is best. I will obey His command and trust that He will still accomplish what I cannot understand."

So he got up; it was a heavy morning for Abraham, but he rose up and went out and prepared for the journey. He got Isaac and two of his servants up and packed up the supplies for the trip. It doesn't tell us that he had a discussion with Sarah about this. He didn't expect her to understand what God had asked him to do; it would appear that he didn't even bother her with the information. He just got up and prepared for the task and set out on the journey.

It wasn't just a few hours away, it was days, and each day as they walked all day long, you know what was on Abraham's mind. You know the heartache that was in his chest. You know the burden that he was carrying. There wasn't a more troubled man on the planet for those three days than Abraham. He was going to make the ultimate sacrifice. It would be harder for me to sacrifice my son than myself. I would gladly give myself in his place, or in any of my children's place. I love them more than my own life.

What a picture that this is also of our Lord; as for three days He took a journey for us. He entered into the pit of hell itself and for three days paid the price for us. And it was for the great love of God that this was done. I cannot imagine the burden on the heart of God the Father as He watched His own son on the cross paying for my sins. I cannot fathom the heartache that it must have caused Him. But, friend, understand that is how much God loves you.

We talk about the law of first mention in reference to Bible interpretation. This is as real as it gets. The first mention of love in the Bible is presented as the ultimate picture of God's love for us, and it is a picture of sacrifice. Love is sacrifice. Love is giving what is dearest to us, what the closest thing is to our heart.

So Abraham arrived at Mount Moriah where he was instructed to go to. The picture got even more beautiful here as we examine the scriptures and find that this was the place where the temple would be built. It says in 2 Chronicles 3:1: "Then Solomon began to build the house of the LORD at Jerusalem in mount Moriah, where the LORD appeared unto David his father, in the place that David had prepared in the threshingfloor of Ornan the Jebusite." That temple, the ultimate picture of the sacrifice of Jesus Christ as they would bring in the sacrifice year after year to offer upon the altar the shed blood, as the high priest would make atonement for the sins of the people. That picture was first made by Abraham and Isaac. One day, the very Son of God would be not only the sacrifice but also the High Priest of our faith, and He would offer His own blood upon the altar. And as He was making that ultimate sacrifice upon the cross, the veil of that temple would be ripped in two, and the access to the Holy of Holies would be forever open to you and me through Him.

This was the opening picture of the plan of God upon Mount Moriah. As they arrived, Abraham took the wood and laid it upon the back of his son Isaac, just as Jesus would take the wood of His own cross and carry it up to Golgotha. Abraham took the fire in his hand and the knife, and both of them went up together into the mount. And as they were ascending, Isaac asked his father, "Behold the fire and the wood, but where is the lamb for the burnt offering? I don't understand, dad, you said we were going to make an offering to the Lord. I see the instruments of the offering; I see the wood, the fire, and the knife. But I don't see an offering. How is this going to work?"

Then we hear one of the most glorious verses in the Bible as Abraham said, "My son, God will provide Himself a lamb for a burnt offering." I cannot imagine Abraham saying that without tears streaming down his face. I cannot imagine his statement without the thought, *I don't know, son, I don't understand why God has asked this. I just believe that somehow, someway, God is going to intervene.* Yet, Abraham was saying something more than even that. I love the Word of God; it is so precise, it is so perfect, because one day God indeed would provide Himself a lamb. He Himself would become the Lamb of God that would take away the sin of the world. How could it be any more clear, God Himself the Lamb. And as John stood at the Jordan river and cried out, "Behold the Lamb of God which taketh away the sin of the world," God had indeed provided himself a Lamb. Abraham's words to Isaac that day were fulfilled in Jesus Christ. I know that Abraham was talking about a physical lamb, but I believe that God was prophesying through him as well when Abraham didn't understand what he was really saying.

Finally, they arrived up to the top of the mountain and began to build an altar there. Stone by stone they laid it up. And then piece by piece they laid the wood in order, and then the hardest part. Abraham then took a rope and began to wrap it around his son. And he bound up Isaac and picked him up and laid him upon the altar. It couldn't have been without weeping. It couldn't have been without questions in the mind of Isaac. We don't read of him questioning, and we don't read of him resisting, but I wonder what it must have been like there at that moment. I imagine that it was a lot like in the garden of Gethsemane, when Jesus sweated great drops of blood and shed many tears and agonized before the Father over the sacrifice that He was to make.

Let me ask you this, if God loved you like this, that He laid down the life of His own son, how can you not receive Him? If you have never received Jesus Christ as your Saviour, how could you reject Him who gave His own life for you? How could you persist in your sin and reject the Saviour?

Furthermore, believer, how could you look at the sacrifice that He made for you and withhold anything from Him? How could you say to Him, "I will not give what you want. I will not submit this to your will"? Abraham put God ahead of the thing that he loved more than anything in this world. He trusted God with his dearest possession. I wonder what God has asked you to trust Him with.

And he raised his hand to take the life of Isaac his son, and the Lord called out to him and said, "Lay not thine hand upon the lad." Make no mistake about it though; God knew that Abraham had offered him up in his heart already. Hebrews 11:17–19 says, "By faith Abraham, when he was tried, offered up Isaac: and he that had received the promises offered up his only begotten son, 18 Of whom it was said, That in Isaac shall thy seed be called: 19 Accounting that

God was able to raise him up, even from the dead; from whence also he received him in a figure."

Abraham believed God! God made the sacrifice of His Son for you. His blood was shed because of your sin. You have violated the law of God and sinned against a Holy and Righteous God, and because of that sin, you deserve to pay the penalty, which is death and eternal separation from God in the lake of fire. But the love of God found mercy for you and paid the penalty for your sin through Jesus Christ's death, burial, and resurrection. He died and was raised for you, and He calls upon you now to turn from your sin and turn from your ways and put your faith and trust in Him to be your Saviour. He requires you to call on Him as Lord! How could you reject such love as He showed to you?

Believer, He is calling on you to put Him first above all else. He may have already asked you for something in your life, and you may have been struggling with giving it to God. Count him faithful as Abraham did, knowing that He was able to raise up Isaac even from the dead to accomplish His will. You will never lose by giving what you cannot keep to gain what you cannot lose. What sacrifice do you need to place on the altar today?

PUT THE PAST BEHIND YOU

And Joseph was brought down to Egypt; and Potiphar, an officer of Pharaoh, captain of the guard, an Egyptian, bought him of the hands of the Ishmeelites, which had brought him down thither. And the LORD was with Joseph, and he was a prosperous man; and he was in the house of his master the Egyptian. And his master saw that the LORD *was* with him, and that the LORD made all that he did to prosper in his hand. And Joseph found grace in his sight, and he served him: and he made him overseer over his house, and all *that* he had he put into his hand. And it came to pass from the time *that* he had made him overseer in his house, and over all that he had, that the LORD blessed the Egyptian's house for Joseph's sake; and the blessing of the LORD was upon all that he had in the house, and in the field. And he left all that he had in Joseph's hand; and he knew not ought he had, save the bread which he did eat. And Joseph was *a* goodly *person*, and well favoured.

Genesis 39:1–6

And it came to pass, when his master heard the words of his wife, which she spake unto him, saying, After this manner did thy servant to me; that his wrath was kindled. And Joseph's master took him, and put him into the prison, a place where the king's prisoners *were* bound: and he was there in the prison. But the LORD was with Joseph, and shewed him mercy, and gave him favour in the sight of the keeper of the prison. And the keeper of the prison committed to Joseph's hand all the prisoners that *were* in the prison; and whatsoever they did there, he was the doer *of it*. The keeper of the prison looked not to any thing *that was* under his hand; because the LORD was with him, and *that* which he did, the LORD made *it* to prosper.

Genesis 39:19–23

The next two chapters of Genesis outline the rise of Joseph from slave to statesman. It takes him from the pit to the palace and shows the amazing grace of God, as well as the providential hand of God in his life. There are few people who have the character that Joseph had, and there are few that have the patience that Joseph had when facing the trials of life. I believe that these two chapters can be a great blessing to us if we will grab hold of the principles that we see in the life of this great man and apply them to our hearts to make them a part of us so that when we face the trials of life, God can get the glory and bless us just as He did with Joseph.

We are going to look at these characteristics one at a time and it is going to take us a few chapters to do it. The first thing that we find out about Joseph in our text is that he was a prosperous man. The word *prosperous* means "advancing in the pursuit of any thing desirable; another definition is "to push forward." We might put it like this: Joseph was a man who didn't spend any time looking behind him. His focus was on what lay before him. He was always looking to advance in the pursuit of things that were desirable.

I tell you, this is a very important characteristic in the life of Joseph. The truth is that most people spend all their time looking the wrong way. Most people spend all their time looking backward instead of forward in their lives. I remember years ago, as a teenage boy, my dad took me out to our farm ground and set me up in the tractor after I had learned to drive it. I was about thirteen or so, and Dad said, "Son you are going to plow this field today, and if you are not careful, your rows will be crooked and you will spend the whole day trying to fix it." I want you to know that you cannot plow a straight row looking backward. You pick out a point on the horizon and you just drive straight to it and you will have a straight row. It was a terrible temptation to look backward, but I want to tell you today there is no way to plow a straight row in life if you are looking backward either.

The only thing that looking backward will get you is a pain in the neck. The course that you and I have to run is ahead of us, not behind us. There are some people who are so preoccupied with what has happened to them that they never are able to be used of God where they are. They are so preoccupied with how things used to be that they are miserable today. The backward looking and bemoaning is a terrible waste of a life. I know of people who haven't lived a day since a tragedy happened in their lives, they are stuck on that day, it dominates their thinking, it pollutes their relationships and their decisions. They are bitter, they are miserable, and they are miserable to be around with.

Let me tell you something. Joseph didn't sit around crying about the fact that he had been sold into slavery. You don't read that he was bitter because he had been separated from his father. There is no time spent on his thinking about the injustice that had been done to him, considering the fact that he had been taken from a comfortable life of ease and forced into a position of slavery or that he was wrongly accused and thrown into prison. Those things were secondary. Joseph didn't ruin his tomorrow because of his yesterday. Some people have chosen to throw away all their tomorrows because of one yesterday, over one event that they just couldn't put away.

But, preacher, you just don't know what it was like. You just don't understand, you have just never been through what I went through. No, I haven't, and there are things that I have been through that you have never been through. There are things that others have gone through that were worse than what you have gone through. The issue isn't what you have gone through; it is how you have responded to it.

Everyone goes through trials and troubles; everyone has problems. Job told us that man is born unto troubles as the sparks fly upward. God allows troubles to come into our lives so that we will understand that sin has consequences. Now, don't tell me that you have never sinned. Don't tell me that you don't deserve trials. The truth is that you have a pride problem. You have an "I" problem; you cannot get your view off of you and on to Him. Maybe God let this trial come into your life so that you would stop looking so much at yourself and start depending on Him instead. But you have allowed it to create a singular focus on you. What a shame, because God is going to have to allow more problems into your life to get your attention.

I want to share with you some things that will help you if you will apply them in this area of moving on from tragedy.

First, you must humble yourself. Our pride is what causes us more problems than anything else when it comes to getting over trials. We really think that we should never have had those problems to begin with. We cannot understand how God could do such a thing to us. Let me help you, He did! God is in control, and He can change the circumstances of life. If you don't believe that, stop praying. God has all the power.

Why does He allow troubles to come? It is so that we will see the terrible consequences of sin, and so that He can show Himself mighty for us. When a person realizes that they are a sinner and they turn to God in godly sorrow, confessing and repenting, God takes the blood of Jesus Christ and applies it to their heart. Now if there was never a problem in your life, you wouldn't understand that you needed His love and forgiveness. You would think that you had it made pretty well on your own. You would say, "I don't need God."

Of course, God allows trials to come in our lives. By the way, He didn't stop it from coming in the life of Jesus Christ Himself. Jesus faced trials, Jesus faced problems, Jesus faced persecution, and even death, and He had never sinned. So don't try to justify yourself to the point that you should never have had a problem because you had never committed any great sin. Jesus had committed absolutely no sin, and yet God allowed a greater trial of affliction to come in His life.

David said of his troubles in Psalm 109:26–30, "Help me, O LORD my God: O save me according to thy mercy: That they may know that this *is* thy hand; *that* thou, LORD, hast done it. Let them curse, but bless thou: when they arise, let them be ashamed; but let thy servant rejoice. Let mine adversaries be clothed with shame, and let them cover themselves with their own confusion, as with a mantle. I will greatly praise the LORD with my mouth; yea, I will praise him among the multitude."

When you acknowledge that it was God's hand in your life that allowed these troubles, you humble yourself to acknowledge that He is God and He can do whatever He wants. If you are His, He is in control, or did you only give Him limited control? Did you only give Him permission to do what you wanted? Either God is Lord of all or He is not Lord at all. Giving Him control takes the power away from the Devil, and it takes the power away from your enemies and causes you to lift up your voice in praise to God, even in trials.

The next thing that you must do is cover it. If you are going to move on after you have humbled yourself, you are going to have to cover the offense before you can move on. Take a look at this account with me quickly in 2 Samuel 20:9–13:

> And Joab said to Amasa, *Art* thou in health, my brother? And Joab took Amasa by the beard with the right hand to kiss him. But Amasa took no heed to the sword that *was* in Joab's hand: so he smote him therewith in the fifth *rib*, and shed out his bowels to the ground, and struck him not again; and he died. So Joab and Abishai his brother pursued after Sheba the son of Bichri. And one of Joab's men stood by him, and said, He that favoureth Joab, and he that *is* for David, *let him go* after Joab. And Amasa wallowed in blood in the midst of the highway. And when the man saw that all the people stood still, he removed Amasa out of the highway into the field, and cast a cloth upon him, when he saw that every one that came by him stood still. When he was removed out of the highway, all the people went on after Joab, to pursue after Sheba the son of Bichri.

There are some events that happen in our lives that cause us to stand still, and there are also some things that are so traumatic that they freeze us in time. We are fixated on them. Now these were men of war, these were men in the midst of a battle, and yet they were frozen from going forward because of the sight of this man wallowing on the ground in his blood as he died. There was nothing that they could do for him, there was nothing that watching it would accomplish. I am amazed at the nature of mankind to just stand and watch a tragedy and just be frozen in time.

That is what has happened to many people. It could have happened to Joseph. He could have been frozen there because of the tragedies that had befallen him, but he made a choice to cover it and move on. He took it out of the highway and moved it off to the field and placed a sheet over it so that it was not in the way of going forward in life. It isn't that it never happened; it is, however, the same principle as dealing with grief. If you are going to go forward in life, you must bury your dead out of your sight.

The event that took place in your life, the reason that you cannot get over it, the reason that it has such a prominent place in your life is that you have never dragged it out of the middle of the highway. You are standing there in the road and holding up everyone around you while you stand still and look at it wallowing in the blood there on the ground. And it is a fruitless existence because you cannot do anything about it, you cannot change it, and you cannot move on until you bury it.

You must, in your heart, pull it off the highway of your life and cast a cloth over it; you must move on. Don't build a memorial to it, don't set up a monument so that you can always remember it. Just cover it and go on. You might say, "But if I just move on, I am dishonoring someone." But no, friend, God is the God of the living.

He has already taken care of the issue from death. The question isn't what will happen to them and the question isn't what has happened to you. But the question is, will you let God be God? Will you put it in His hands and cover it and say, "God, I don't understand why that happened, but I know that You have a purpose. So I am going to cover it so that it doesn't hinder me from going on."

Then you must forget it. Paul probably put it better than anyone in Philippians 3:13–14: "Brethren, I count not myself to have apprehended: but *this* one thing *I do*, forgetting those things which are behind, and reaching forth unto those things which are before, I press toward the mark for the prize of the high calling of God in Christ Jesus." We have a task before us. We do not have time to be focused on the troubles of yesterday, and if we are going to move on to the high calling of God in our lives, we must forget about the things that are in the past.

But, preacher, I just cannot forget about it. No, you choose to not forget about it. You forget other things all the time. You forget about good things all the time, it is this bad thing that you won't put away and forget about. Friend, it is as Paul said, if you are going to go on for Christ, that thing must be forgotten. The word *forgetting* means "to lose or to neglect." You must let it loose from your focus, set it free from your grip. You must then neglect it, don't allow it to be your focus anymore. As you do this, you will find that you don't remember it like you used to. It will drift off into the hazy place of memory past, and it will not have the pain that it once did. It will not have the power that it once did, and you will, at length, be free from it completely.

Part of this is not just forgetting, but reaching forward for the things that are before. Have you noticed this pattern, cover it and move on, forget it and reach forward. God has a great promise lying just in front of you, but if you don't move you will never receive it. You must set the thing loose and then neglect it. There is no profit for your life in holding it so tightly. Holding on cannot bring peace, only more sorrow.

But how can you just forget? You forget by reaching for something else and neglect to hold on to it anymore. Change your thinking; as long as you dwell on it in your thinking, you will be held there. Philippians 4:6–8 tells us: "Be careful for nothing; but in every thing by prayer and supplication with thanksgiving let your requests be made known unto God. And the peace of God, which passeth all understanding, shall keep your hearts and minds through Christ Jesus. Finally, brethren, whatsoever things are true, whatsoever things *are* honest, whatsoever things *are* just, whatsoever things *are* pure, whatsoever things *are* lovely, whatsoever things *are* of good report; if *there be* any virtue, and if *there be* any praise, think on these things."

The word *careful* here means "full of care, consumed by care over a problem or trial." Be careful for nothing—that includes the problem that you are fixated on right now. Instead, pray and put it into God's hands so that He can give you peace in place of the burden. And then make a conscience decision to control your thinking. God tells us in 2 Corinthians 10:3–6: "For though we walk in the flesh, we do not war after the flesh: (For the weapons of our warfare *are* not carnal, but mighty through God to the pulling down of strong holds;) Casting down imaginations, and every high thing that exalteth itself against the knowledge of God, and bringing into captivity every thought to the obedience of Christ; And having in a readiness to revenge all disobedience, when your obedience is fulfilled." You can choose to capture those thoughts and bring them into obedience to Christ. You can choose to think on things that are true, honest, just, and pure. You can choose to think on things that are lovely and of a good report. You can choose to think on things that are virtuous and praiseworthy rather than the trouble that you have had. You are the only one who can make that choice. Nobody is holding you there but you.

Be prosperous. How can someone move on from tragedy in their life? How could someone just get up the next day and move on? You mean if you were, say, sold into slavery by your own brothers and you were taken to a strange land and a man bought you and brought you to his house and said, "Work, slave," how could you do it? You mean if you were being a diligent worker and someone falsely accused you of something, and there was no trial and there was no evidence, and everyone just believed the lies to the point that you were thrown into prison and locked up in a dungeon, how could you deal with that?

You only must make the decision to be prosperous in life. You must decide like Joseph did—pursue what is desirable and decide to push forward. But I just can't, and then you will be punished. I can't, and then you will be miserable. You don't see a miserable person here in Joseph; instead, you see a man who humbled himself and covered the offenses and forgot about them and changed his thinking to be prosperous. That is a choice that you can make. Now, what choice will you make?

WALK WITH GOD

Last chapter, we started looking at the thought of how to seize triumph from tragedy, and we saw the importance of putting the past behind us and reaching forward to the future that God has prepared for us. Now I want to notice another characteristic that Joseph exhibited as he seized triumph in his life. A brief mention of this is made at the beginning of the last chapter—that Joseph had a fervent relationship with the Lord.

Notice what it says here in these passages:

> "And the LORD was with Joseph, and he was a prosperous man; and he was in the house of his master the Egyptian" (Genesis 39:2).

> "And his master saw that the LORD *was* with him, and that the LORD made all that he did to prosper in his hand" (Genesis 39:3).

> "And it came to pass from the time *that* he had made him overseer in his house, and over all that he had, that the LORD blessed the Egyptian's house for Joseph's sake; and the blessing of the LORD was upon all that he had in the house, and in the field" (Genesis 39:5).

> "But the LORD was with Joseph, and shewed him mercy, and gave him favour in the sight of the keeper of the prison" (Genesis 39:21).
>
> "The keeper of the prison looked not to any thing *that was* under his hand; because the LORD was with him, and *that* which he did, the LORD made *it* to prosper" (Genesis 39:23).

You might look at these verses and say, no wonder Joseph had a great relationship with God. Look at what all God did for him. But I submit to you that what God did for him was a result of the kind of relationship that Joseph had with the Lord. Furthermore, I submit to you that God wants to have that same kind of relationship with you, and God wants to bless you just as much as He ever has any of His children. Isn't it funny that we can see a man like Joseph and how God blessed him and say, well, obviously he was one of God's favorites, but forget the terrible circumstances he was in? Remember, he was a slave, he was in prison, these were not the most convenient places. I have never seen someone in prison and thought, well, obviously God loves them, look how He is blessing them. Yet, we will do that with Joseph because we know how the story turns out.

What I am saying is that the reason this story turns out differently from so many is because of the fervent and intense personal relationship that Joseph had with God. I want to share with you, this idea of how to have a fervent personal relationship with God and how to have the blessing of God in your life. There are many passages in the Bible that we could look at on this topic (the entire Bible is a road map to having a fervent relationship with God). But the one passage that, to me, contains a very clear and direct path is found in Proverbs 3:1–12:

My son, forget not my law; but let thine heart keep my commandments: For length of days, and long life, and peace, shall they add to thee. Let not mercy and truth forsake thee: bind them about thy neck; write them upon the table of thine heart: So shalt thou find favour and good understanding in the sight of God and man. Trust in the LORD with all thine heart; and lean not unto thine own understanding. In all thy ways acknowledge him, and he shall direct thy paths. Be not wise in thine own eyes: fear the LORD, and depart from evil. It shall be health to thy navel, and marrow to thy bones. Honour the LORD with thy substance, and with the firstfruits of all thine increase: So shall thy barns be filled with plenty, and thy presses shall burst out with new wine. My son, despise not the chastening of the LORD; neither be weary of his correction: For whom the LORD loveth he correcteth; even as a father the son *in whom* he delighteth.

This passage in particular has instruction and promise wrapped together in a concise and direct manner that we can see just how each of us can have the kind of relationship with God that Joseph had. Let's look at it in this manner—first the instruction, and then the promise, of which there are six of them.

Instruction: Keep my commandments. (verse 1)

Often we say the phrase "keep my commandments," but I want you to see today the process of that in this passage; it begins with the statement, "Forget not my law." If you are going to keep the commandments of God, you must begin by preparing your mind to do so. Too often the mouth will say, "I want to do this, I want to follow God." I have heard many a person tell me, "Preacher, I want to do what God wants," but then they don't follow through on that. It isn't long and they are out in the world, walking in the flesh. I don't believe that they were lying. At that moment, they really did want to follow God, but they failed in one of the first and most important areas—they didn't conform their thinking to accomplish that task.

Paul says of some in Romans 1:28, who were found in the throws of extreme wickedness, "And even as they did not like to retain God in *their* knowledge, God gave them over to a reprobate mind, to do those things which are not convenient." They determined to pursue the desires of their flesh, and in order to do that they could not retain God in their knowledge. They had to push the thoughts of Him and His Word and commandments out of their mind. Friend, let's be real today. There are times that sinfulness and the lust of the flesh enter into your mind, and you know that the law of God is against it. But rather than remembering His law, you push it out of your mind. At those moments, you do not like to retain God in your knowledge and you intentionally forget His law. I am telling you today that if you are going to keep His commandments, it begins with firmly establishing your mind in the truth and setting up barriers to forgetting it. You will never consistently walk with God until you have established your mind in His law.

The Scripture also says here, "let thine heart keep my commandments." Notice that before the hands keep God's commandments, the mind and the heart must be settled in them. It is from the heart that we are to walk in His way. It is not about the duty of our hands, it is about the love of our heart. Jesus said, "If you love me, keep my commandments." David said, "Thy Word have I hid in mine heart that I might not sin against God." Keeping the commandments of

God is a heart issue. The Bible tells us in Ezra 7:10: "For Ezra had prepared his heart to seek the law of the LORD, and to do *it*, and to teach in Israel statutes and judgments." Oh, how we need to prepare our minds and hearts to seek the law of God. You cannot keep His commandments without preparing these areas.

Jesus said in John 14:23–24 "Jesus answered and said unto him, If a man love me, he will keep my words: and my Father will love him, and we will come unto him, and make our abode with him. He that loveth me not keepeth not my sayings: and the word which ye hear is not mine, but the Father's which sent me." The issue of keeping His commandments is not purely an action issue. If you have narrowed your Christian life down to just do and don't, you will be miserable and you will fail. The issue is a heart and mind issue. The issue is if you love God not just with your words and actions but within the depths of your heart so that you have set your mind upon Him and fixed your heart upon Him. If you have done this, you will keep His commandments.

If you have prepared your mind and your heart, and you are serving God from love rather than duty, it is not a burden to follow His commandments. I want to tell you today, I have found by experience that it isn't hard to follow His Word when you love Him. It isn't a struggle to obey Him when you love Him.

Promise: Long life and peace (verse 2)

What a joy that when we do love Him and obey His commandments, He gives us such peace as we can never know without Him. The Psalmist in Psalm 119:165 said, "Great peace have they which love thy law: and nothing shall offend them." This world has such a longing for peace, but they are seeking it in the wrong places and the wrong way. Making everything fair, according to your definition of fairness, will never bring you peace; there will always be inequality. Taking from one person and giving to another will never create peace. Some think getting rid of religion would bring peace, but they don't understand the basic nature of man. Everyone worships something; even those who deny God are worshiping something. True peace only comes through keeping God's commandments because of a true heart based love for Him.

Instruction: Keep mercy and truth. (verse 3)

Two things it seems that are lacking in many people today are these two areas of mercy and truth. Here we are not speaking of God's mercy to us but rather our mercy to others. Do you understand that Christians are to be full of mercy for others? We are to demonstrate the mercy of God for others. Often, for some reason, we are eager to show others justice but reluctant to show them mercy. We want them to understand that we know how to judge, but we are so lacking in the demonstration of mercy to others. God help us, how is it that we have so twisted ourselves up that we don't understand mercy?

God didn't give us what we deserved. We stand in the church house and say, "I am so glad for the mercy of God that He saved me when I was a poor wretched sinner. And then we go out and condemn those who trespass against us, and those who are wounded, we look down on and sneer at as if we were never in sin. God help your wretched soul for that wickedness. The problem often is that you don't realize just how much mercy God has shown to you. You have forgotten just how wicked you were—or are now. I mean to tell you, when I look at the mirror of God's Word, I am amazed that there is enough mercy in heaven to forgive me. But then, how far should I fall short of that mercy when I cannot find enough mercy in my heart to forgive another of some simple offense against me?

God said that we are to keep mercy—that is, we are to show it, demonstrate it, and lavish it upon others just as God has lavished it upon us. We are also to keep truth. God does not sacrifice truth for mercy, He doesn't excuse away our sin, He never said it didn't matter. What He said was, "You are guilty and it has a penalty, but I want to show you mercy, and if you will acknowledge the truth, I will." We are told by God to buy the truth and sell it not, we are told to bind it to us. We are to hide it in our hearts and keep it before our eyes; we are to put it on the doorposts of our house, and it is to be our guidepost; we are to hate lies and deceit. You cannot build your life upon lies and deceit. It may seem that people get away with lies for a while, but God always turns the table on them; they will not get away with it forever. It is vital that we keep truth, both concerning keeping the Word of God and keeping ourselves in truth in our daily lives, and walk among people.

Promise: Favor and good understanding with God and man (verse 4)

When we show mercy to others, we receive back favor and understanding from them. A few years ago, I moved my family out to the country and we lived on a couple acres where we are able to have farm animals. I really love the idea of being self-sufficient and having a farm, so we started our own little farm with pigs, goats, cows, turkeys, and lots of chickens.

It was a great learning experience. One of the things that I found in starting the farm, is that farmers respond in kind to what you show them. If you are kind and honest, if you are generous, then that is what you get back. If you lie and are crooked, if you are trying to get one over on them, I have seen them shut people down fast. They are skeptical about people, but once they have seen that you are honest and kind, they will bend over backward to help you. I have seen this issue of keeping mercy and truth work and have received favor and good understanding back from men. How much more then if we receive that same thing from God.

Instruction: Trust in the LORD with all your heart, and lean not unto thine own understanding. (verses 5–6)

Here we are back to this heart and mind issue. First, God said, "Conform your mind and heart to love me and then you will follow my commandments." Now He is saying, "Don't revert back to your old way of doing things when there is trouble. Stop trying to figure out another way to deal with problems, trust in the Lord, Stop depending on your own understanding, and trust me. Stop trying to solve your own problems and trust me." How much clearer can the Lord make it than that? Just trust me."

I remember when my kids were little, I would take them and put them up on something and say, "Jump and I will catch you." As young children, they would jump without a moment's hesitation. But as they got older, though I had never dropped them, their faith in my ability to catch them began to diminish. It is an awful lot like that in the Christian life as well. God hans't changed, but we have a tendency to stop trusting Him. We have a tendency to lean on our own thinking and forget just how great and mighty He is. He tells us to jump, and we back away and doubt that He can catch us. We have a faith problem when it comes to walking in His will.

We say, "God, show me what to do. God, show me your will." "Preacher, I just don't know what God's will is." The reason that we are struggling isn't because God has hidden His will from us, it is because we have refused to follow what He has told us to do. We have questioned and second-guessed it because it seemed to contradict with what we wanted to do, or we thought that God cannot possibly want us to do what He has told us to do.

God may have spoken to you about being a witness to someone, and you might have said, "God, I cannot do that," or responded like Moses did, "I am not a good speaker, God." Maybe God called you to be a preacher or a missionary, and you have said, "But, Lord, you don't understand. I am too old," or "I am too young," or "I am not a good fit for that, Lord, you must be mistaken."

Friend, God called Joseph to be a servant in Egypt, and it didn't make sense to say that to the natural man. Yet, God put him there and said, "Joseph, just trust me." God put him in prison, and it didn't make sense. If you were going to devise a plan to save Israel from famine, you wouldn't say, "First, you have to be a servant and then you have to go to prison." But then God knows all things, just trust Him with all your heart. Don't worry about your own understanding.

Promise: He shall direct thy paths. (verse 6)

What a great promise, if you will trust Him, He will direct your paths. You want to know God's perfect will for tomorrow? Do what He said today.

Instruction: Be not wise in thine own eyes, fear the Lord, depart from evil. (verse 7)

We live in a day in which evil is promoted as good. The sin of our society is seen as wisdom instead of wickedness. *Depart* means "to leave undone, to turn aside, or remove from." We must not engage in sin, we must abstain from sin. It says in 2 Timothy 2:19: "Nevertheless the foundation of God standeth sure, having this seal, The Lord knoweth them that are his. And, Let every one that nameth the name of Christ depart from iniquity." It also says in 1 Peter 2:11: "Dearly beloved, I beseech *you* as strangers and pilgrims, abstain from fleshly lusts, which war against the soul;" The wisdom of this world is actually foolishness God tells us in Romans 1:22 "Professing themselves to be wise, they became fools."

Let me tell you that we see this principle active in the life of Joseph. We will speak more about it in the coming chapters, but day by day he was faced with the temptation of lust by a wicked woman. Joseph was obviously an attractive man. She may not have been the only offer to do wickedly that he had, but every day Joseph turned away from the evil that was before him. He walked in the wisdom of the Lord rather than in the pride of his heart and the lust of his flesh.

Too often we walk into evil rather than away from it. We pursue sin rather than flee from it. God says in 2 Timothy 2:22: "Flee also youthful lusts: but follow righteousness, faith, charity, peace, with them that call on the Lord out of a pure heart." We are told to depart from evil in Proverbs, and Paul said to flee from lust, not just to not do it but really run away from it, refuse to leave it before your eyes to be a temptation.

Promise: Health (verse 8)

The word *navel* here not only means your belly button, but also the center of your strength. In other words, God promises to heal your inner man if you will depart from evil. As well as going on to say marrow to thy bones. The bone marrow produces your blood cells. If you have healthy marrow, you will have a healthy body. What a promise. God gives if we will depart from evil. Let me say that doesn't mean that God will never allow sickness into our lives. Sometimes, He does for His glory, but when He does, refer back to the verse, "Trust in the Lord with all thine heart and lean not unto thine own understanding. In all thy ways acknowledge Him and He shall direct thy path." God can take care of us and bless us, even in sickness.

Instruction: Tithe (verse 9)

I like the way that this is worded, "Honor the Lord with thy substance, and with the first fruits of all thine increase." Let's break that down just a minute, it says "all thine increase." That means that we are to give based upon the gross of our income. God wants us to remember Him above all else. We should not support our government before we honor our God! We should not fund our retirement before we honor our God! It says "with the first fruit," God says our tithing is not to be an afterthought; God is to be first on our mind and heart at all times. That means when we go on vacation, we are still to give the first of our increase to Him. That means when it gets close to Christmas, we are to give the first of our increase to Him. That means when we get an extra blessing, we give the first of that increase to Him.

The scriptures put it like this: "Honor the Lord with thy substance." Now God says, "I have given it to you, it is yours to do what you will with, but I would like you to remember who it was that gave it to you, and honor me with it." To tithe is to give honor to God, to not tithe is to dishonor God. No wonder He curses us when we don't tithe, we have dishonored Him. Listen, tithing is not something that was commanded just under the law, it was instituted before the law by the faith of Abraham. It was practiced by all the patriarchs before the law and commanded by Jesus in the New Testament. God never changed the fact that people of faith were to honor God with their giving!

A tithe is not just what I have left; it is the first tenth of what I receive. If I am paid ten dollars per hour, the first dollar of that is the Lord's. I taught my family that it isn't a question of if we will tithe; we always honor God first. When my kids got money from somewhere, the first thing they always did was to come up to Angela and me and ask us to break the bill down so they could pull out their tithe before they did anything else. I was so glad; I wanted them to learn to honor God first.

Promise: Provision (verse 10)

God promises that He will take care of our provision if we will honor Him. Now, you can struggle to get by without Him, or He can provide for you if you will honor Him. I cannot understand how it works all the time, but I know this: it always works. Not only that, but He also promises blessing on top of provision. It says not only will your barns be filled with corn, but your presses will burst out with new wine. I want you to know that God wants to bless you, but if you don't honor Him with your substance, He cannot not. You put the hindrance upon God because He will not violate His Word.

Instruction: Receive correction. (verse 11)

Finally, here we are to humble ourselves under the correction of God. We are not to despise it, and we are not to be weary of it. We are not to get to the point where we say, "I am so tired of God working in my life. I just wish He would leave me alone." Why is God doing it? Because He is trying to correct your thinking and your direction so that He can bless you with abundant blessings. He is working to mold you and change you into His image, and the only way to do that is to correct your steps.

I have to keep my eye on the fact that God is always desiring for what's good for me. He wants the best for me. If I rebel against His correction in my life, then I will suffer. If I bow my neck up and stiffen my will against Him, I will suffer. He wants to bless me. He wants me to be happy, but He also knows that true happiness doesn't come when a person is self-willed. It doesn't come when a person is arrogant and proud. It doesn't come when we are rebellious to authority or when we puff up at correction. Peace comes when we humble ourselves to receive correction, and when we yield ourselves to chastening, accepting it as God working in our lives to better us.

Our spirit about correction is important. Most often with my children, I work more with their spirit toward correction than the issue of correction. I mean, a child bows up and stiffens against it, they don't want to be corrected, they want to do it their way, they want to be left alone, but God wants them to submit to authority in their life. Joseph is a great example of this; God was correcting him and molding him, and it took some hard things to do that in Joseph's life, but what we see is that he humbled himself to God in all those steps. He didn't bow up and say, "If you are going to treat me like this when I am serving you, then I quit." He didn't say, "Stop it, God, I am done, I won't go any further with you now." No, he submitted to God, and God blessed him over and over again.

Promise: Delight (verse 12)

The Bible says here that God does this for the son that He loves. Do you realize that if God didn't love you, He would never correct you? He would just let you go on to destruction in your life and let you press on to pain and sorrow. But because He loves you, He wants you to have a blessed life. He is just like a father when He loves his son; when he sees the promise and ability to excel in his own son, he delights in his son and wants him to be blessed. He wants him to know the joy of success in his life rather than failure. I want God to delight in me. I want my heavenly father to be pleased with my life. You can see in our text in Genesis that God delighted in Joseph, God was with Him, and God blessed all that he did.

Why? Because Joseph followed these principles and had the right kind of relationship with God. It was no accident that God blessed Joseph the way that He did. It was because Joseph was humble to God and honored Him above all. When God is first in your life, He can make you an example of blessing to others so that they will see just how God wants their life to be as well.

So how is your relationship with God? How is your walk with Him? Are you walking like Joseph did so that God can bless you, even when you are facing trials? Are you keeping your heart right so that he can show Himself strong on your behalf, or have you allowed trials to hinder your walk with Him? Have you allowed yourself to bow up and rebel against His working in your life? Why not humble yourself to Him today and begin to develop that right relationship with Him that you should have?

BE DILIGENT IN THE BUSINESS THAT GOD GIVES YOU TO DO

Over the last few chapters, as we have looked at this idea of how to seize triumph from tragedy, we have learned from the life of Joseph that you first must put the past behind you and move forward in what God wants you to do. Secondly, we learned that we must walk with God in a real and fervent relationship. Now I want to focus on a third characteristic that we see in Joseph that I believe God used in bringing him through this time of tragedy in his life.

The thing I want to notice is found in Genesis 39:4–6:

> And Joseph found grace in his sight, and he served him; and he made him overseer over his house, and all *that* he had he put into his hand. And it came to pass from the time *that* he had made him overseer in his house, and over all that he had, that the LORD blessed the Egyptian's house for Joseph's sake; and the blessing of the LORD was upon all that he had in the house, and in the field. And he left all that he had in Joseph's hand; and he knew not ought he had, save the bread which he did eat. And Joseph was *a* goodly *person*, and well favoured.

I believe it would be appropriate to say that Joseph was a diligent man. As you look through the examples given of his life, there is no doubt that it didn't matter if it was as a slave, as a prisoner, or as the second-in-charge of the kingdom; Joseph was diligent in everything that he did. The word *diligent* means 1) steady in application to business; constant in effort or exertion to accomplish what is undertaken; assiduous; attentive; industrious; not idle or negligent; applied to persons, and 2) steadily applied; prosecuted with care and constant effort; careful; assiduous; as, make diligent search.

Diligence is an attribute that is severely lacking in our culture. We seem to have devolved into a general sense of apathy about mostly everything. The common phrase I believe is "meh." I don't really care, I don't really want to be here, I don't really want to give any effort beyond breathing at this point. People approach their jobs in this way. They approach their studies in this way. There are vast swaths of people in our day whose whole life seems to be an attempt to get through life without ever having to do anything at all.

As a matter of fact, about the only thing that we, as a people, seem to be diligent about is entertaining ourselves with frivolous and useless pursuits. If you get a group of people together, they are going to likely speak of sports, movies, or video games, depending upon their ages. The goal of most in life has devolved into a grand pursuit of useless and frivolous activity. No wonder we have been taught that we are here by some cosmic accident and there is no God, no supreme purpose to life, and we are going nowhere.

The general lack of diligence is not surprising, seeing that the vast majority of people in our day are practical atheists in their thinking. Let me clear that up for you just really quickly. There is a God who created the heavens and the earth, and He created man for a purpose. He was there when you were formed and has a purpose for your life, which extends beyond what sports you like, beyond hellywood, and the zombie box, er, Xbox.

God told Jeremiah in Jeremiah 1:5, "Before I formed thee in the belly I knew thee; and before thou camest forth out of the womb I sanctified thee, *and* I ordained thee a prophet unto the nations." I want you to hear me loud and clear—God didn't love Jeremiah more than you, he just listened more than you. God formed you as well, He knows you, brought you forth, and sanctified you to a purpose. He has ordained you to a special place of service that only you can fulfill, so quit wasting your life with emptiness.

Stop saying, "Someday when I have an important job, I will be diligent." Stop saying, "Someday when I grow up…" or "Someday when my talents are recognized…" or whatever else excuse you are using to be lazy now. Get a hold of this truth, that if you are going to be blessed by God, you must cultivate diligence in your life. I believe that God blesses busy people. I don't believe in luck, I believe that diligent people find themselves in the right place because of the providence of God. There may be times when a person just finds himself in the right place at the right time, but more often than not, it is that diligent person who, because of hard work and preparation, finally met the right time. Luck is often where diligence met opportunity.

Listen to the contrast that God makes between being diligent and being lazy in Proverbs 10:4: "He becometh poor that dealeth *with* a slack hand: but the hand of the diligent maketh rich." I know that it is popular in America to think that those who are rich just happened into it and thus diminish the idea of hard work as a source of reward. I know that the idea of capitalism is condemned now rather than celebrated because we are moving toward a socialistic entitlement society (I read the other day that the number of people on food stamps exceeds the combined population of twenty-four entire states). Laziness has taken hold of the hearts of many, and in order to justify their sin, they sneer and mock diligence. But the

Bible still says in Proverbs 12:24, "The hand of the diligent shall bear rule: but the slothful shall be under tribute." Lazy people complain about authority but are not diligent enough about their affairs to be worthy of authority. Diligent people are elevated to authority because they can be depended upon to finish the job.

Proverbs 12:27 says, "The slothful *man* roasteth not that which he took in hunting: but the substance of a diligent man *is* precious." Diligent people are not wasteful with their resources. They use what they have to the fullest extent that it can be used, but the slothful and lazy person puts off their work. They procrastinate and don't prepare for their future needs, thus they are often in need. That same principle is shown in Proverbs 13:4: "The soul of the sluggard desireth, and *hath* nothing: but the soul of the diligent shall be made fat." And again in Proverbs 21:5: "The thoughts of the diligent *tend* only to plenteousness; but of every one *that is* hasty only to want." We are told in Proverbs 27:23, "Be thou diligent to know the state of thy flocks, *and* look well to thy herds." Not long ago in our family devotions, we read this verse, "Seest thou a man diligent in his business? he shall stand before kings; he shall not stand before mean *men*" (Proverbs 22:29). A lazy and slothful man often reaps anger from others for their wickedness, but a diligent man is often rewarded with promotions.

Now, all of these things have to do with our secular activities. These things have to do with what kind of employee we should be, what kind of life we should live, and how we should conduct our affairs. The Bible affects every area of our life. God just told you how to get a promotion, how to be set financially, and how to have sufficient provision. God has given unto us all things that pertain to life and godliness. This is the way in which diligence pertains to life in general, but in 2 Peter, God tells us how diligence pertains to us spiritually, how it pertains to godliness when it says, "*Seeing* then *that* all these things shall be dissolved, what manner *of persons* ought ye to be in *all* holy conversation and godliness, Looking for and hasting unto the coming of the day of God, wherein the heavens being on fire shall be dissolved, and the elements shall melt with fervent heat? Nevertheless we, according to his promise, look for new heavens and a new earth, wherein dwelleth righteousness. Wherefore, beloved, seeing that ye look for such things, be diligent that ye may be found of him in peace, without spot, and blameless" (2 Peter 3:11–14).

Peter says we know that the Lord is coming again, that this earth is going to be dissolved, and that there is not going to be anything left here. All the footballs, basketballs, and baseballs, all the theaters and televisions, all the video games and controllers are going to be burned up; all the trees and mountains will be burned up, and all that will be left will be us and God. Now seeing that we know this is true, Peter says it seems then that we should be diligent about being found by God in the right way. What he is asking is that when Christ returns, how will He find you? Will He find you fully engaged in frivolous and lazy slothful activity, or will he find you diligent about the things that He has given you to do?

First, Peter references this, will the Lord will find you in peace. The scriptures are clear that without Him, there would be no peace. Ephesians 2:14 says, "For he is our peace, who hath made both one, and hath broken down the middle wall of partition *between us*." We are told in Colossians 1:20: "And, having made peace through the blood of his cross, by him to reconcile all things unto himself; by him, *I say*, whether *they be* things in earth, or things in heaven." If there has never been a time that you trusted Him as your Saviour, then He will not find you in peace; He will find you in condemnation for your sin. We are told in John 3:18: "He that believeth on him is not condemned: but he that believeth not is condemned already, because he hath not believed in the name of the only begotten Son of God." And Jesus said in John 14:27: "Peace I leave with you, my peace I give unto you: not as the world giveth, give I unto you. Let not your heart be troubled, neither let it be afraid." And again in John 16:33: "These things I have spoken unto you, that in me ye might have peace. In the world ye shall have tribulation: but be of good cheer; I have overcome the world."

Paul explained how to attain this peace in Romans 5:1: "Therefore being justified by faith, we have peace with God through our Lord Jesus Christ." Peace with God only comes through faith in the Lord Jesus Christ. It doesn't come through good works, though good works will follow our faith. It doesn't come through religion, though pure religion is a symptom of true faith. However, faith is experiential; it is a personal investment of the belief of your heart and mind into the acceptance of the truth of the scriptural account of the death, burial, and resurrection of Jesus Christ for the payment for your sin. Seeing others trust Him by faith isn't enough to get you there. You must put your faith in Him personally.

In April 1988, the evening news reported on a photographer who was a skydiver. He had jumped from a plane along with numerous other skydivers and filmed the group as they fell and opened their parachutes. On the film shown on the telecast, as the final skydiver opened his chute, the picture went berserk. The announcer reported that the cameraman had fallen to his death, having jumped out of the plane without his parachute. It wasn't until he reached for the absent ripcord that he realized he was freefalling without a parachute. Until that point, the jump probably seemed exciting and fun, but tragically, he had acted with thoughtless haste and deadly foolishness. Nothing could save him, for his faith was in a parachute never buckled on. Faith in anything but an all-sufficient God will be just as tragic spiritually.

There are many who are freefalling through life with faith in something that will not catch them. The Bible says in Philippians 2:12: "Wherefore, my beloved, as ye have always obeyed, not as in my presence only, but now much more in my absence, work out your own salvation with fear and trembling."

Peter goes on to say in his explanation of what we should be diligent in spiritually, "Be diligent that ye may be found of him in peace, without spot, and blameless." Paul uses this term "spot" in reference to the coming of Christ as well in Ephesians 5:27 "That he might present it to himself a glorious church, not having spot, or wrinkle, or any such thing; but that it should be holy and without blemish." What he and Peter are referring to is holiness, living a holy and pure life. This present manifestation of Christian living that we see in our day, where you can be just like the world and still consider yourself holy, is a lie from hell. The Bible is clear that the standard of holiness is not set by hellywood; it is set by God. It isn't set by what your friends say is acceptable but by God. Peter said, 1 Peter 1:14–16 "As obedient children, not fashioning yourselves according to the former lusts in your ignorance: But as he which hath called you is holy, so be ye holy in all manner of conversation, Because it is written, Be ye holy; for I am holy."

"Without spot" means that you are diligent to keep yourself out of sin. That doesn't mean that you will always be successful, but it does mean that when you commit sin, you confess and forsake it. It means that you and I are to be diligent to purify ourselves and live a holy life. To do that, we must forsake those things that hinder holiness. There are things in my life that I have gotten rid of because when I have them around, it causes me to wander into sinfulness. I am diligent about what I listen to, what I watch, who I am around with, and where I go, because I don't want to put myself into a situation that I am going to be enticed into sinful behavior. I want to be holy.

I don't always succeed, but I want to be without spot. I want to be pleasing to my God. I want Him to find me being diligent about my walk with Him. This present "Meh" mentality about holiness is troubling when you consider the commandment of God and the standard that He set as being His own Holiness.

Peter also said there that we are to be diligent to be blameless. Blameless doesn't carry the same idea of just holiness but rather diligence in performing the ministry that God has called us to do. Consider what it says in 1 Corinthians 1:4–8: "I thank my God always on your behalf, for the grace of God which is given you by Jesus Christ; That in every thing ye are enriched by him, in all utterance, and *in* all knowledge; Even as the testimony of Christ was confirmed in you: So that ye come behind in no gift; waiting for the coming of our Lord Jesus Christ: Who shall also confirm you unto the end, *that ye may be* blameless in the day of our Lord Jesus Christ." And Philippians 2:14–16, which tells us, "Do all things without murmurings and disputings: That ye may be blameless and harmless, the sons of God, without rebuke, in the midst of a crooked and perverse nation, among whom ye shine as lights in the world; Holding forth the word of life; that I may rejoice in the day of Christ, that I have not run in vain, neither laboured in vain."

Being blameless indicates that you have served faithfully in the calling of ministry. Now each of us who are saved has a calling to serve God. Some are called to be pastors or missionaries, some to be evangelists, some to be Sunday school teachers or deacons, but all are called to serve the Lord. All are called to be witnesses; all are called to be faithful. Do you see the aspect of spiritual diligence here? You are to be diligent to make sure that you are in Christ and saved, and then you are to be diligent to keep yourself pure and live a holy life. And finally, you are to be diligent to do what God has called you to do in serving Him. There is to be fervency about it, there is to be a focus with the whole heart, not giving into the present day spirit of laziness. We don't need lazy and slothful Christians; God wants fervent and diligent children who will serve Him and press into the Kingdom with fervor. Brethren, let us, like Joseph, be diligent in all our endeavors, both secularly in our employ and spiritually in our walk with God.

RESIST TEMPTATION

And it came to pass after these things, that his master's wife cast her eyes upon Joseph; and she said, Lie with me. But he refused, and said unto his master's wife, Behold, my master wotteth not what *is* with me in the house, and he hath committed all that he hath to my hand; *There is* none greater in this house than I; neither hath he kept back any thing from me but thee, because thou *art* his wife: how then can I do this great wickedness, and sin against God? And it came to pass, as she spake to Joseph day by day, that he hearkened not unto her, to lie by her, *or* to be with her. And it came to pass about this time, that *Joseph* went into the house to do his business; and *there was* none of the men of the house there within. And she caught him by his garment, saying, Lie with me: and he left his garment in her hand, and fled, and got him out. And it came to pass, when she saw that he had left his garment in her hand, and was fled forth, That she called unto the men of her house, and spake unto them, saying, See, he hath brought in an Hebrew unto us to mock us; he came in unto me to lie with me, and I cried with a loud voice: And it came to pass, when he heard that I lifted up my voice and cried, that he left his garment with me, and fled, and got him out. And she laid up his garment by her, until his lord came home. And she spake unto him according to these words, saying, The Hebrew servant, which thou hast brought unto us, came in unto me to mock me: And it came to pass, as I lifted up my voice and cried, that he left his garment with me, and fled out.

Genesis 39:7–18

We have seen three characteristics in Joseph, so far, that caused him to be able to seize triumph from tragedy. We saw that he was willing to put the past behind him and reach for the things that God had for him now. He had a fervent and personal relationship with God and was diligent in the things that he was given to do. The next major characteristic that we see in Joseph is that he knew how to resist temptation. Someone once said, "I can resist anything, except temptation."

What is temptation? Dwight Pentecost explained it as the "seduction to evil, solicitation to wrong. It stands distinguished from trial thus: trial tests, seeks to discover the man's moral qualities or character; but temptation persuades to evil, deludes, that it may ruin. The one means to undeceive, the other to deceive. The one aims at the man's good, making him conscious of his true moral self; but the other at his evil, leading him more or less unconsciously into sin. God tries; Satan tempts."

Often when we fall into sin because of temptation, we have a tendency to blame God for allowing it to happen. The Bible says in James 1:13, "Let no man say when he is tempted, I am tempted of God: for God cannot be tempted with evil, neither tempteth he any man."

Philip Yancey in his book, *Reaching for the Invisible God*, describes the way God gets blamed for things in this way: When Princess Diana died in an automobile accident, a minister was interviewed and was asked the question, "How can God allow such a terrible tragedy?" and I loved his response. He said, "Could it have had something to do with a drunk driver going ninety miles an hour in a narrow tunnel? Just how exactly was God involved?"

Years ago, boxer Ray "Boom Boom" Mancini killed a Korean opponent with a hard right hand to the head. At the press conference after the Korean's death, Mancini said, "Sometimes, I wonder why God does the things he does."

In a letter to Dr. Dobson, a young woman asked this anguished question, "Four years ago, I was dating a man and became pregnant. I was devastated. I asked God, 'Why have you allowed this to happen to me?'"

Susan Smith, the South Carolinian mother who pushed her two sons into a lake to drown and then blamed a fictional carjacker for the deed a couple years ago, wrote in her confession: "I dropped to the lowest point when I allowed my children to go down that ramp into the water without me. I took off running and screaming, 'Oh, God! Oh, God, no! What have I done? Why did you let this happen?'"

Just because God does not supernaturally intervene to stop you from yielding to the temptation of sin, doesn't mean that He let something happen. He gave you a free will and gave us the tools in His Word to keep ourselves from yielding to temptation. Here in our text, God gave us an example of just how to do that. Temptation comes in many forms, but the answer of how to overcome it is the same in every case. Let's take a close examination of what Joseph did in the Scriptures to see what we can do in gaining victory over temptation.

The trap of temptation is laid in Genesis 39:7: "And it came to pass after these things, that his master's wife cast her eyes upon Joseph; and she said, Lie with me." Here is a young man who, because of his work, was put in a situation where he was responsible to serve Potifar's wife, who was a harlot, a wicked woman, and adulterous. The Bible says in Proverbs 6:26: "For by means of a whorish woman *a man is brought* to a piece of bread: and the adulteress will hunt for the precious life." That verse describes this woman to perfection. Sexual immorality was likely common in Egypt as it was a pagan culture, but it was still not accepted, as is seen by the fact that Joseph was cast into prison based upon her accusation. Here she is, enticing him to sin, trying to convince him, and yet we see the first thing that Joseph did, the Bible says that he refused, and that is not something that we often consider. The first step to overcoming temptation is to just refuse to do it.

Refuse to do wrong. Joseph had made up his mind, before this had happened, that he was going to walk with God. He had already determined that he was not going to defile himself, and because he had already made that covenant with God, he didn't have to think about it. He didn't have to weigh the options, he didn't consider the consequences. "Man, if I don't do what she says, she may lie about me," he said. "I am not going to do this. We don't need to discuss it, we don't need to contemplate it. The decision is made, and I refuse."

You need to just make up your mind that you are not going to do wrong. You need to quit letting our situational ethics society cause you to be uncertain about what is right and wrong. Wrong is wrong, and there is no compromise with it if you are going to walk with God. Job said in Job 31:1, "I made a covenant with mine eyes; why then should I think upon a maid?" I think that it is interesting the way that this is worded. There is a direct relationship given here between looking with your eyes and what you think about. The longer that you look, the more you think about doing it. Joseph refused and didn't stay around to look and contemplate. He didn't spend his time thinking about it. He brought his thoughts into captivity to the obedience of God and said, "I will not do this, I will not look at it and think about it. The answer is no."

The problem that we often have is that we have eyes that are full of adulteries. We are looking at it, and because we are looking, we are thinking about it as well. Our thoughts are filled up with sinfulness. We are rehearsing the possibilities in our minds and feasting on the temptation with our eyes, and then we blame God when we yield to it. It isn't God's fault if you yield to temptation, it is yours. It isn't God's fault if you refuse to control your eyes, it isn't God's fault if you refuse to control your thoughts. It is time to make a decision that you will not involve yourself with the filth of this world and just commit yourself to that and stop standing around like a kid at the candy counter lusting after what you know you are not to have.

Remember your responsibility. Genesis 39:8 says, "But he refused, and said unto his master's wife, Behold, my master wotteth not what *is* with me in the house, and he hath committed all that he hath to my hand." Sin is also always a forsaking of your responsibilities. When a man allows himself to be overtaken in lust, he is shirking his responsibility to his wife and children. He made a vow to be faithful to his wife. He, by nature of being a father, is responsible to set a right and godly example to his children.

Stealing from your employer is breaking the responsibility that you have to be honest with them in the trust that they have invested in you. Stealing from anyone else is a violation of the social contract that we have with one another that makes our society work. Honesty is the bedrock of any civil society. You understand that Joseph knew that his responsibilities were more important than his desires. We live in a day in which desire trumps obligation. We deny ourselves nothing that is wanted. We are so used to just indulging all of our lusts, that the idea that we would consider our responsibilities before our lusts is odd to most thinking.

Whatever thought of wickedness that comes into the mind is indulged in; the covenants that we have made and the responsibilities that we have take a backseat to the lusts that we have. This was not the case for Joseph. His first concern was that this sin would break the trust that he had with his master and violate his responsibilities. There should be a great fear within us to forsake our responsibilities. Mark Twain said, "There are several good protections against temptation, but the surest is cowardice," that meaning the fear of being found out to have broken the trust of those nearest to us.

Next, you must refocus on your opportunities. Genesis 39:9a says, "*There is* none greater in this house than I; neither hath he kept back any thing from me but thee, because thou *art* his wife." If your remember back in Genesis 3, one of the tactics that the Devil used was to twist the words of the Lord and say God has said that you cannot eat of all the trees in the garden. Notice the difference in what Joseph said, "neither hath he kept anything from me but thee." Satan wants us to look at the object of sin; God wants us to look at the opportunity of life. There are so many things that I can do, why would I want to do the one thing that is forbidden? There is so much good that I can experience, why jeopardize that for the one bad thing? In the garden, there were thousands of trees, and for the sake of one, they sinned. So it is in life; there are so many opportunities to do good, yet we allow our focus to be turned to the one sinful thing that we are forbidden, and it consumes our thinking until we indulge and are punished.

Joseph had the right prospective of life. Someone once said that faith is seeing things from God's perspective. If we are going to have faith enough to gain victory over temptation, we must also keep our view as God's view in this area. He has given every good thing for us and loved us with a great love that provided for all of our needs and great blessings for us.

Then we must realize what yielding to temptation is. Genesis 39:9b says, "How then can I do this great wickedness, and sin against God?" It isn't just a mistake, it isn't my personal preference, it is sin. We are too adept at renaming sin and making it more palatable. We don't want to call it drunkenness, we want to call it a disease. We don't want to call it sodomy, we want to call it an alternative lifestyle. We don't want to call it adultery, we want to call it personal gratification or some other nonsense to justify it. But it is sin, it is wicked, it is breaking God's holy law.

David, when confessing his sin, said in Psalm 51:2–4, "Wash me throughly from mine iniquity, and cleanse me from my sin. For I acknowledge my transgressions: and my sin *is* ever before me. Against thee, thee only, have I sinned, and done *this* evil in thy sight: that thou mightest be justified when thou speakest, *and* be clear when thou judgest." Every sin, be it great or small in the eyes of men, is ultimately against God and God alone. It is a violation of His law and His righteousness. It is a mark against our souls in the books of God.

Brethren, if we could get this down in our souls, if we could get it firmly planted in our minds and the minds of our children, we would be better able to withstand temptation. We live in a day when the wicked have socially engineered our schools to teach our children that they are animals, that they are more responsible to polar bears than to God, that saving the earth is the greatest cause and saving a soul is fanaticism. George Bush first brought the new world order teaching into our school system in 1992 with the adoption of the United Nations agenda 21 propaganda. It has been fully implemented in the minds of our children right before our eyes. But it began before believers allowed their children to be taught that "evil-lution" was a fact rather than a lie. Then they were indoctrinated in sex education by the school system because parents shirked their responsibilities. When we abdicated the Word of God, we gave up the truth, and we are reaping the reward of that error today in our culture, and it has affected even the people of God whose thinking has been affected as well. All the while we think that we have our own minds, but we have adopted the same wicked style of thinking that is polluting our children's minds.

Friend, God hates sin, God hates it because He knows what it will do to you. He knows how much it will cost you because He Himself has already paid the price. He knows how painful it is. He loves you so much that He hates the sin that will destroy your life and damn your soul to the Devil's hell. Before you can be forgiven, you must acknowledge that you have sinned against Him and turn your heart to Him in repentance.

Next, you must flee from temptation. Genesis 39:12 says, "And she caught him by his garment, saying, Lie with me: and he left his garment in her hand, and fled, and got him out." Someone once said that when you flee from temptation, be sure you don't leave a forwarding address. Listen to what the Bible says about this idea of fleeing from temptation in 1 Corinthians 6:18: "Flee fornication. Every sin that a man doeth is without the body; but he that committeth fornication sinneth against his own body."

Paul warns us in the Scriptures to flee from a number of things. In 1 Corinthians 10:14, he says, "Wherefore, my dearly beloved, flee from idolatry." In 1 Timothy 6:11, he also tells us, "But thou, O man of God, flee these things; and follow after righteousness, godliness, faith, love, patience, meekness." And then again in 2 Timothy 2:22, "Flee also youthful lusts: but follow righteousness, faith, charity, peace, with them that call on the Lord out of a pure heart." That is a lot of fleeing that we have to do; we are to flee from fornication, flee from idolatry, flee from sinful behavior, and flee from youthful lust. So where should we flee to? David tells us in Psalm 143:9, "Deliver me, O LORD, from mine enemies: I flee unto thee to hide me."

Charles Spurgeon said: "What settings are you in when you fall? Avoid them. What props do you have that support your sin? Eliminate them. What people are you usually with? Avoid them. There are two equally damning lies Satan wants us to believe: 1) just once won't hurt 2) now that you have ruined your life, you are beyond God's use and might as well enjoy sinning. Learn to say no. It will be of more use to you than to be able to read Latin."

BE A SERVANT

And it came to pass after these things, *that* the butler of the king of Egypt and *his* baker had offended their lord the king of Egypt. And Pharaoh was wroth against two *of* his officers, against the chief of the butlers, and against the chief of the bakers. And he put them in ward in the house of the captain of the guard, into the prison, the place where Joseph *was* bound. And the captain of the guard charged Joseph with them, and he served them: and they continued a season in ward. And they dreamed a dream both of them, each man his dream in one night, each man according to the interpretation of his dream, the butler and the baker of the king of Egypt, which *were* bound in the prison. And Joseph came in unto them in the morning, and looked upon them, and, behold, they *were* sad. And he asked Pharaoh's officers that *were* with him in the ward of his lord's house, saying, Wherefore look ye *so* sadly to day? And they said unto him, We have dreamed a dream, and *there is* no interpreter of it. And Joseph said unto them, *Do* not interpretations *belong* to God? tell me *them*, I pray you. And the chief butler told his dream to Joseph, and said to him, In my dream, behold, a vine *was* before me; And in the vine *were* three branches: and it *was* as though it budded, *and* her blossoms shot forth;

and the clusters thereof brought forth ripe grapes: And Pharaoh's cup *was* in my hand: and I took the grapes, and pressed them into Pharaoh's cup, and I gave the cup into Pharaoh's hand. And Joseph said unto him, This *is* the interpretation of it: The three branches *are* three days: Yet within three days shall Pharaoh lift up thine head, and restore thee unto thy place: and thou shalt deliver Pharaoh's cup into his hand, after the former manner when thou wast his butler. But think on me when it shall be well with thee, and shew kindness, I pray thee, unto me, and make mention of me unto Pharaoh, and bring me out of this house: For indeed I was stolen away out of the land of the Hebrews: and here also have I done nothing that they should put me into the dungeon. When the chief baker saw that the interpretation was good, he said unto Joseph, I also *was* in my dream, and, behold, *I had* three white baskets on my head: And in the uppermost basket *there was* of all manner of bakemeats for Pharaoh; and the birds did eat them out of the basket upon my head. And Joseph answered and said, This *is* the interpretation thereof: The three baskets *are* three days: Yet within three days shall Pharaoh lift up thy head from off thee, and shall hang thee on a tree; and the birds shall eat thy flesh from off thee.

Genesis 40:1–19

As we continue on in our study of Joseph and how to seize triumph from tragedy, I notice a very important thought that we often overlook in our trials. The characteristic that we are going to focus in on is that of being a servant.

Often in the face of trials, we become very self-focused. We are concerned about what is happening to us. We analyze and re-analyze and become so focused on us that we forget about everyone around us or marginalize their problems, holding ours up as the greatest problems that have ever been. Because of that, we have a tendency to become depressed and sink into despair.

Joseph was able to maintain a spirit of joy through the midst of the hard trials he was going through. He didn't deny, however, that there were problems. I want you to notice what he says to the butler in Genesis 40:14–15: "But think on me when it shall be well with thee, and shew kindness, I pray thee, unto me, and make mention of me unto Pharaoh, and bring me out of this house: For indeed I was stolen away out of the land of the Hebrews: and here also have I done nothing that they should put me into the dungeon."

Joseph wasn't in denial about the problems that he was having, he was realistic about them. He was normal and wanted out of them, but he wasn't allowing them to be the focus of his existence. He had made the decision to move forward and be prosperous in spite of the problems. One of the keys to doing this was his service to others. Let's consider how Joseph served.

First, he served with joy. Here, Joseph was in the same situation as these men; he had been there longer and was there unjustly. Yet as he walked in one morning to serve these men, Genesis 40:6–7 described it as: "And Joseph came in unto them in the morning, and looked upon them, and, behold, they *were* sad. And he asked Pharaoh's officers that *were* with him in the ward of his lord's house, saying, Wherefore look ye *so* sadly to day?" Joseph was of such a nature to live in joy, that he thought it was strange that these two men who had been servants in the palace would be sad in the prison. He asked why they looked so sad. He didn't know about their dreams at that point, he only knew about their countenance.

Your countenance says a lot about your heart. Notice the following verses: "And the LORD said unto Cain, Why art thou wroth? and why is thy countenance fallen?" (Genesis 4:6). "And she said, let thine handmaid find grace in thy sight. So the woman went her way, and did eat, and her countenance was no more *sad*" (1 Samuel 1:18). "The wicked, through the pride of his countenance, will not seek *after God*: God *is* not in all his thoughts" (Psalm 10:4). "*It is* burned with fire, *it is* cut down: they perish at the rebuke of thy countenance" (Psalm 80:16). "A merry heart maketh a cheerful countenance: but by sorrow of the heart the spirit is broken" (Proverbs 15:13).

Dudley Hall said, "Countenance is a press conference that your face calls to give the state of union of your soul." Joseph was focused on the needs of others and could tell by their countenance when they had a problem. The other day, I went to the store to grab something, and the clerk was obviously troubled about something. I said, "Your day must not be going well," and she replied that it was not and was surprised that it showed on her face. I gave her a tract and told her I would be praying for her. I wonder how many opportunities to share the Lord we might have passed up because we are not attentive to the countenance of those around us. When you see someone with a troubled countenance, that is the perfect time to give a witness of the hope that is in the Lord.

Joseph was not in the same state as these men, though they were in the same circumstances. They were sad, he had joy. The difference was not the circumstances; the difference was their hope. The butler and baker had no hope because their hope was based upon men. Joseph had hope because his hope was based in the Lord. Often, the reason that we lose our joy is because we forget that God is in control. In the darkest night, in the worst of the trials, He is still in control. You can still trust Him, even when you don't understand what is going on and when you don't see how things can work out, you can still depend on Him and He will see you through. That is why, as a believer, you can have joy, even when the world has sorrow. That is why you can have peace, even when the world has fear.

Listen to how we are instructed to face the trials in 1 Thessalonians 5:18: "In every thing give thanks: for this is the will of God in Christ Jesus concerning you." Philippians 4:4 also says, "Rejoice in the Lord always: *and* again I say, Rejoice." You might say, "But, preacher, you don't understand how bad it is." No, you don't understand how big God is. "But, preacher, I have already prayed, and God didn't answer." No, you have just come to the point that He wants you at to see if you really trust Him or not. If you trust Him, you won't give in to the sadness and fear. If you trust Him, you will abide in His joy and peace, even in the dungeon, because we know that He is still in control.

It was once said that joy is the byproduct of obedience. Apostle Peter expressed this concept of joy in trials when he said in 1 Peter 1:6–9: "Wherein ye greatly rejoice, though now for a season, if need be, ye are in heaviness through manifold temptations: That the trial of your faith, being much more precious than of gold that perisheth, though it be tried with fire, might be found unto praise and honour and glory at the appearing of Jesus Christ: Whom having not seen, ye love; in whom, though now ye see *him* not, yet believing, ye rejoice with joy unspeakable and full of glory: Receiving the end of your faith, *even* the salvation of *your* souls."

We can rejoice in trials so that one day, when He appears, we might be found able to give Him all glory and honor and praise, for He has brought us through. Rejoice, rejoice, there is to be joy in the trial knowing that it is an opportunity to prove the faithfulness of God for you. If, however, you are doubtful of your relationship with Him, then your lack of joy is understandable.

I want you to notice another thing that Joseph did in this trial—he took the time to point others to Christ. Notice what he said to them upon hearing about their dreams: "And they said unto him, We have dreamed a dream, and *there is* no interpreter of it. And Joseph said unto them, *Do* not interpretations *belong* to God? tell me *them*, I pray you" (Genesis 40:8). Often in our trials we become so focused on our problems that we fail to speak to others about God's solutions. What better time to point people to the Lord than when they can see our faith at work. It is good to point people to Christ when things are good, but when things are bad and we give the testimony that God is still good, that has an impact on others. Joseph was saying that God had the answers to their fears. God has the answer to your fears and trials.

Sharing our faith should be so woven into the fabric of our being as believers, that it is what comes to the surface when life is turned upside down. That which is most prevalent in your heart will come to the surface when your life is stirred up. It will reveal whether Christ is the center of your life or just a mere accent. Sadly, witnessing has been relegated to "what they used to do" section of Christianity Yet, it was the last commandment of our Lord as He said in Acts 1:8, "But ye shall receive power, after that the Holy Ghost is come upon you: and ye shall be witnesses unto me both in Jerusalem, and in all Judaea, and in Samaria, and unto the uttermost part of the earth."

A 1980 Gallup poll of evangelical Christians found that only 2 percent of professing believers had ever led someone else to Christ. Someone said that the Gospels record Jesus having personal contact with 132 individuals. Of that, six were in the temple, 4 were in the synagogue, and 122 were in the mainstream of life. How often do we wait and delay and fail to ever point another to Jesus Christ?

In the 1800s, distinguished lawyer Samuel Hoar (1778–1856) was representing a defendant. When it was time to present his case, he told the jurors that the facts favoring his client were so evident that he would not insult their intelligence by arguing with them. The jury retired to deliberate and returned in a few minutes with a verdict of guilty. Samuel Hoar was astonished! "How," he asked, "could you have reached such a verdict?" The foreman replied, "We all agreed that if anything could be said for a case, you would say it. But since you didn't present any evidence, we decided to rule against you." Silence had lost the case.

Friends, millions are lost because of silence. It is our lack of sharing Christ that has condemned our nation to the state that it is in, and condemned millions of souls to hell. And all the while, God is trying to get our attention, and we wonder why the trials come our way. I tell you, often these trials are an opportunity to share the love of God with others, if we will take it. There is no greater time to show Him than when life seems to have no sense of reason or hope. Paul and Silas, who were in jail in Philippi and bound in chains, did not fail to sing of God's love. And when the place was shaken, they saw a great conversion of the jailer at the moving of God. Multitudes were converted because Paul, despite his trials, consistently told of Jesus Christ. God may have put that trial in the right place to cross your path with someone who was ready to hear the truth of salvation.

Finally, I want you to see that even in the midst of the trial, Joseph was a man who always spoke the truth. As he began to interpret the dreams for these two men by the aid of the Lord, one interrelation was life, but the other was death. Joseph spoke the truth to each man. People today need the truth. They need someone who is bold enough to tell them the truth. If you are not speaking the truth to them, you are found a false witness. Too many have passed over the hard truths and glossed over the problems to try and make people feel good, not knowing that, in the act, they're only condemning them to hell.

In a survey conducted a few years ago, 51 percent of respondents said that they did not witness because of fear of how others would react. They did not tell them the truth because they were afraid they would be upset. How do you think they will feel as they are cast into hell? God has not given us a spirit of fear! God wants us to speak the truth to those around us. God wants us to get our eyes off ourselves in the trials and realize that there are others who are in far worse condition if they are without Christ. Our burdens may last for a while, but the judgment of sin is eternal. I have never met a sad soul winner. God has a great reward of joy waiting for you if you will put your view on the lost and get it off yourself.

LEARN PATIENCE

Genesis 40:20–41:46

A number of our college-aged people, and some others who are still in the throes of their formal education, are blessed regularly with the delightful event in education known as semester finals. Even when we come across test questions that seem simple on the surface, we find that they're often not as simple as we first thought they would be. For instance, the answer to the question "How long did the Hundred Years' War last?" seems obvious, but the answer is 116 years. When a test asks, "Which country manufactures Panama hats?" the correct answer is Equador. Here's another: From what animal do we get cat gut? The answer is, from sheep and horses, of course. In which month do Russians celebrate the October Revolution? The answer is November. What was King George IV's first name? Well, everyone knows it was Albert. Ah, yes, many test takers are glad to be out of school, to be far away from trick questions like that, thought up in some teacher's lounge.

But as far as we try to get from the rigors of the academic life, we find that our lives are filled with other kinds of tests. We take driver's tests, drug tests, polygraph tests, sobriety tests, eye tests, entrance exams. People in law enforcement have to qualify on the shooting range at least four times a year; many of you have to take a test for your chosen profession. Like it or not, tests are a part of life, and to face these tests, it takes a tremendous amount of patience.

The life of Joseph was full of tests and trials. This is our sixth and final chapter on the topic of how to seize triumph from tragedy as we look at the life of Joseph. Let me just restate the lessons that we have learned from Joseph so far.

1. Put the past behind you and choose to be prosperous today.
2. Walk with God.
3. Be diligent about the business that God has given you to do.
4. Resist temptation.
5. Be a servant.

Now we are going to consider the necessity of learning patience. As we have looked through these passages, we found in Genesis 37:2 that Joseph was around the age of seventeen when he was sold into slavery. By the time we reach this passage, he was already thirty years old. For thirteen years, he was a slave, and for a good portion of that, he was also a prisoner. Nearly half of his life had been spent in unjust captivity. When he saw a glimpse of hope that he would have a way out through the butler who was restored to the palace, he was left for another two years forgotten in the dungeon. As time passed, the hope that he may have had the first few days and weeks faded as they turned into months and years. I am sure that by the time two years had passed, Joseph had given up hope that the butler would ever fulfill his promise to remember him to Pharaoh.

Proverbs 13:12 tell us that "Hope deferred maketh the heart sick: but *when* the desire cometh, *it is* a tree of life." Joseph's hope had been deferred for years, and it might seem possible that, by this time, he would have been sinking down into the abyss of despair. Yet, we do not see that presented in the Scriptures; rather, we see a man ready to rise to the challenge presented to him, still in fellowship with God, and able to direct others to Him. Consider the testimony that Pharaoh gave of him as he said in Genesis 41:38–39: "And Pharaoh said unto his servants, Can we find *such a one* as this *is*, a man in whom the Spirit of God *is*? 39 And Pharaoh said unto Joseph, Forasmuch as God hath shewed thee all this, *there is* none so discreet and wise as thou *art.*"

The level of patience that Joseph had learned in the midst of his trials is astounding. I must say that there is no one that I believe I have ever met who has had anywhere close to that level of patience and grace exhibited in their life. The Webster's 1828 dictionary defines patience as "the suffering of afflictions, pain, toil, calamity, provocation or other evil, with a calm, unruffled temper; endurance without murmuring or fretfulness. Patience may spring from constitutional fortitude, from a kind of heroic pride, or from Christian submission to the divine will."

Patience is more than just being willing to wait, it is waiting with joy. It means cheerful endurance. Often our willingness to wait is tempered with the demeanor of a grizzly bear. Our countenance says, "I will wait, but you will know that I am not happy about it, and if you get too close, I may snap your head off." Margaret Thatcher said, "I am extraordinarily patient, provided I get my own way in the end."

We make sure that God knows that we are waiting, and everyone else knows that we are not pleased with Him about it. Yet, repeatedly, we are told in the Scriptures the importance of adding patience into our life. In Peter's list of the graces of Christian maturity that are necessary to maintaining a fruitful life, he says, "And to knowledge temperance; and to temperance patience; and to patience godliness" (2 Peter 1:6). Patience is one of the eight elements given by him that are vital to add into our life. In Luke 21, when Jesus was speaking of the great trials that would come upon Israel during the tribulation period, he said, "In your patience possess ye your souls" (Luke 21:19). The only way to escape some trials of life is by learning patience.

Solomon in his wisdom said in Ecclesiastes 7:8: "Better *is* the end of a thing than the beginning thereof: *and* the patient in spirit *is* better than the proud in spirit." You and I can say amen to that. There are many times that I have thought to myself, *Man, I am glad that is over.* If you are lifted up in pride during a trial, you will be crushed by the trial, but if you are humbled in patience, you will find endurance that brings you through in peace. That is what Joseph found. Even after thirteen years of bondage, even after thirteen years of injustice, he had learned patience in his life, that his joy was intact, and his heart was preserved in peace.

Consider with me the problem with patience. The main problem with patience is the way in which it must be obtained. It is no secret that patience is acquired through the endurance of trials. We are told in James 1:3, "Knowing *this*, that the trying of your faith worketh patience." Paul reinforces this in Romans 5:3 when he said, "And not only *so*, but we glory in tribulations also: knowing that tribulation worketh patience."

How many times have you heard the statement, "Don't pray for patience because you will get trials"? It is no secret that the only path to patience is through the fire of adversity. God knew this and recorded it for us, yet still instructed us as to our need for it. God could have made it easier to acquire, He could have made it a by-product of salvation; but He chose to make it into something that was only accessible through the trials of life, which we dread so much.

We dread the thought of patience so much because it goes against our goal-oriented lifestyle. We are taught to set goals and press for them, to never be satisfied until we attain what we desire. Yet, patience is achieved by the thwarting of our desires. It is perfected in the hindrances of our goals. The great problem is learning to be content in the circumstances that God has placed you in, without giving up on the vision that He has placed in your heart. Patience is not giving up, it is not lying down and surrendering to never finish what you were striving for; rather, it is persisting with joy when there seems to be no end in sight to accomplish what you are seeking. Yet, patience itself has a promise that is given to us in the Bible. Listen to what God says about the promise of patience. As I looked at the Scriptures, I saw eight things that patience is intended by God to do in our life.

Learning patience will help you obtain what you have waited for. It says in Hebrews 6:12, "That ye be not slothful, but followers of them who through faith and patience inherit the promises." And in Hebrews 6:15, "And so, after he had patiently endured, he obtained the promise." God, in order to teach us this much-needed grace, will hold off that which we are longing for until it produces in us the patience that we need. This is not to punish us but to better us, to make us more perfect and change us into His image. Remember, it is God's desire to mold us into the image of Jesus Christ, thus teaching us patience is an integral part of that conforming process.

1. *Learning patience will help you to be drawn closer to God.* The Bible tells us in Psalm 119:67–68, "Before I was afflicted I went astray: but now have I kept thy word. Thou *art* good, and doest good; teach me thy statutes." In Psalm 119:71, it says, "*It is* good for me that I have been afflicted; that I might learn thy statutes." If we received everything that we longed for immediately, we would not draw close to God. I am not saying that we should draw close to Him to get what we want, but I am saying that the wickedness of our hearts

is such that we already fail to draw close to Him, even when we are struggling most often. It is God's earnest desire to have an intimate personal relationship with us. Yet, though the Creator and Sustainer of this universe, who Himself died to pay the penalty for our transgressions and redeemed us from our iniquity, longs to have a closeness with us, we are so full of selfish pride that we spend our time pursuing meaningless entertainment for our flesh. How wicked we are. It is fortunate for us that God is longsuffering and merciful. Thank God for trials that help us learn to draw close to Him in patience.

2. *That you will know the power of Christ in your life.* In 2 Corinthians 12:9, it says, "And he said unto me, My grace is sufficient for thee: for my strength is made perfect in weakness. Most gladly therefore will I rather glory in my infirmities, that the power of Christ may rest upon me." When we draw close to God, we have a happy side effect. He rests His power upon us. How interesting it is that Paul said, "I will gladly choose the trial if it means that the power of Christ will be in my life."

I dare say that most believers have never grown to that point. Most are in a constant pursuit of getting out of trials rather than glorying in them. Our perspective is backward.

Suffering is part of God's purpose in our lives, not just to teach us patience, but also to allow us to learn peace, joy, and meaning. The Bible tells us that we are to look at the example of Jesus in this: "Looking unto Jesus the author and finisher of *our* faith; who for the joy that was set before him endured the cross, despising the shame, and is set down at the right hand of the throne of God" (in Hebrews 12:2). The suffering in the cross brought joy to Jesus Christ. He is not a masochist. He is trying to show us that true joy comes as the result of overcoming suffering, not avoiding it. Have you ever seen the joy on the face of an athlete who has labored with sweat and tears, often striving to blood, to win the prize? When they attain victory, though their body is exhausted, though they have spent their physical and emotional energy giving everything that they have to the cause, when they win, the sense of jubilation overrides the exhaustion of their body, and they raise their hands in victory and then they leap. The joy of victory comes across their face. Why? Because of the suffering that it took to achieve. It was the suffering that made the feat of more value and taught them joy. Victory that costs you nothing is not valued as much. The reward at the point of suffering, for the believer, is the power of Christ that rests on you when you are yielded to Christ in the midst of trials. It is at that point that you can know something that none other can, what it is like to have a supernatural power strengthening you and lifting you above the trial that would otherwise destroy you. Paul said, "I would rather know that than avoid the trial because there is a joy of victory that I would otherwise never experience."

3. *That you will be perfected in your Christian life.* It says in James 1:4, "But let patience have *her* perfect work, that ye may be perfect and entire, wanting nothing." The word *perfect* here means "to be a complete man of full age," or we might also say "to be a mature person in Christ." It is good to be mature. We often like to act immature and irresponsible, but there is a peace and comfort that comes with maturity. The other thing that comes with maturity is the blessing of responsibility. Immature people are always wanting responsibility, but when they get it, they don't use it properly. They shirk it and demonstrate why they were

not worthy to have it to begin with. There is a blessing that comes with responsibility that a mature person knows. It is God's desire to grow us to spiritual maturity so that He can depend on us to carry out His will in our lives, so that we are dependable and usable. An immature person cannot be trusted with anything of importance. However, when you grab hold of maturity and know the joy of knowing that you have been trusted with the important business of your superior, there is a satisfaction that fills your heart and mind. God wants to do that in our lives, and so He uses trials to perfect us unto patience and to make us perfect and mature.

4. *So that you can do the will of God.* Look at Hebrews 10:36: "For ye have need of patience, that, after ye have done the will of God, ye might receive the promise." In 1 Peter 2:20, it also says, "For what glory *is it*, if, when ye be buffeted for your faults, ye shall take it patiently? but if, when ye do well, and suffer *for it*, ye take it patiently, this *is* acceptable with God." Thomas a Kempis described that kind of patience in these words: "He deserves not the name of patient who is only willing to suffer as much as he thinks proper, and for whom he pleases. The truly patient man asks (nothing) from whom he suffers, (whether) his superior, his equal, or his inferior...But from whomever, or how much, or how often wrong is done to him, he accepts it all as from the hand of God, and counts it gain!" What a powerful statement, what a true thought! I wonder how often in the midst of trials the thought, that you are doing this to accomplish the will of God, comes to your mind. Or are you only interested in doing the will of God when it corresponds with your own will? Are you only interested in doing His will when you think there is some temporal gain in it? Is it not enough to

do the will of God for God's sake? Are we so unspiritual that God's will is only the means to our own end? His will should be done because He is God, He is worthy of our obedience, and we need to obey for His sake. This pleases God better than our feeble sacrifices. When Saul came back from the battle with the Amalekites, God was displeased with him, though he had done most of what he was told to do. He was supposed to destroy everything that pertained to the Amalekites, including their livestock, but he thought it best to bring back the best of them for a supposed sacrifice to God. God said through Samuel the prophet, however, that it is better to obey than to sacrifice. That is the essence of faith; faith is little more than obedience to God. That is what pleases God, and without it, it is impossible to please Him.

5. *To increase your hope and understanding of God's love.* It says in Romans 5:3–5, "And not only *so*, but we glory in tribulations also: knowing that tribulation worketh patience; And patience, experience; and experience, hope: And hope maketh not ashamed; because the love of God is shed abroad in our hearts by the Holy Ghost which is given unto us." It is through the trials that we learn what hope really means. Hope for a believer is much different than it is for the lost man. Some time ago, I was on a plane and engaged in a discussion about the Lord with an agnostic man next to me. He was appalled that we as believers were so foolish about this idea of hope. He said, "You are just full of this empty hope that everything will work out okay." I shared with him that what we mean by hope is different. I do not hope that the Lord will return as a child who hopes he becomes a superhero. My hope is based upon God's Word and His Holy Spirit's presence within me confirming that it is true; thus, my hope is not wistful but substantive. The more that

tribulation works patience in you, the more experience that you have with the presence of God as the Holy Spirit sheds God's love in your heart. Thus, the more hope that you have because you know the power and presence of God's love. I find constant comfort in the love that is present when I am with my wife. Just her presence with me is strengthening to my heart. The same is true with the Lord, and yet to a greater degree. When I am yielded to the Spirit of God, there is a comfort and a strength that surpasses even that of what I sense with my wife near. Her love though is strengthening and temporal, but God's is immortal; His eternal love surpasses that of all others.

6. *To make you fruitful.* Luke 8:15 says, "But that on the good ground are they, which in an honest and good heart, having heard the word, keep *it*, and bring forth fruit with patience." In the last few years, I have taken up gardening. It is a joy to see the labor and hope that are put into a garden come forth into the victory of fruitfulness. Each seed that is planted requires a special care that must be given for it to be most fruitful. Some yield fruit quickly and some take more time. Some yield one fruit and some many, but each one has a special value that makes it beneficial. Within our lives, the seeds of trial are much the same way. Each trial plants a seed that, if we respond properly, will grow up to a beneficial fruit in our lives. That fruit strengthens those who bear it, nourishes those with whom it is offered up to, and is an offering of sweet savor to the Lord.

To teach you true happiness. Such truth is shared in James 5:11, which says, "Behold, we count them happy which endure. Ye have heard of the patience of Job, and have seen the end of the Lord; that the Lord is very pitiful, and of tender mercy." What a thought that we count them happy which endure. It is contrary to this world to think that

Job, after all that he endured, was happy from it. It is, however, the example that God uses to show us the happiness that comes from enduring trials. This also shows us the truth about God's intentions in trials, the fact that God allowing us to go through trials is Him showing pity and tender mercy to us for us to grow and learn what happiness really is.

Finally, I want you to notice the practice of patience. How can we learn this noble attribute and add it into our lives as we were instructed in 1 Peter?

Through attendance to the Scripture. It says in Romans 15:4: "For whatsoever things were written aforetime were written for our learning, that we through patience and comfort of the scriptures might have hope." It often takes patience to gain the comfort of the Scriptures. You might not gain the comfort that you seek with a casual or brief reading of the Bible, but if you diligently peruse the comfort of the Lord through attendance to the Scripture, you will find it as God adds patience into your life through His Word. The Bible is full of examples of God bringing people through trials. Testing is a normal part of life, and we can see that played out in the accounts recorded in the Scriptures for us. Through attendance to these accounts, we can learn the truths that will help us to navigate the rough water of tribulation in life.

Through dependence upon God. It shows us in Colossians 1:11: "Srengthened with all might, according to his glorious power, unto all patience and longsuffering with joyfulness." It may seem odd to say that patience comes through our dependence on God; however, that is what the Scriptures tell us. In essence, it is the practice of dependence on God that little by little adds patience into our lives. We are to be in a constant state of learning patience as our dependence moves from our own flesh to the power of God. Dependence on our own abilities is what so often gets us into trouble, and yet so often we persist in our own way. Faith is trusting in God's ability rather than our own. Faith moves us from the realm of our abilities to the realm of God's abilities, and with God nothing is impossible. Trials help us see more clearly that we cannot make it without God, and the patience that we learn through that helps us to walk by faith rather than by sight.

Through laying aside the weight of sin in our lives. As we see in Hebrews 12:1: "Wherefore seeing we also are compassed about with so great a cloud of witnesses, let us lay aside every weight, and the sin which doth so easily beset *us*, and let us run with patience the race that is set before us."

George Matheson wrote, "We commonly associate patience with lying down. We think of it as the angel that guards the couch of the invalid. Yet there is a patience that I believe to be harder—the patience that can run. To lie down in the time of grief, to be quiet under the stroke of adverse fortune, implies a great strength; but I know of something that implies a strength greater still: it is the power to work under stress; to have a great weight at your heart and still run; to have a deep anguish in your spirit and still perform the daily tasks. It is a Christ-like thing! The hardest thing is that most of us are called to exercise our patience, not in the sickbed but in the street." To wait is hard; to do it with "good courage" is harder!

I don't know why it is so hard for the old nature to be put down, but it is. Sin is so deceptive and powerful in our lives. As a young believer, I often got frustrated with myself and condemned myself because of my seeming inability to put sin out of my life. The old accuser is good at putting us in that situation, but through patient and diligent perseverance in truth, little by little, we learn the truths from God's Word that help us to lay sin aside in our lives. This is a marathon, not a sprint. Those who learn that lesson best are the most successful in their Christian life because the issue of patience is a maturity issue. The more sin that you lay aside, the more patience you add to your life and the more maturity that you develop.

We can add patience through obedience to God's commandements as well. It says in Revelation 14:12: "Here is the patience of the saints: here *are* they that keep the commandments of God, and the faith of Jesus." That couldn't be more clear, could it? Our patience consists in just keeping the commandments of God. When things are going wrong, patience says just keep doing what you know God has said to do. That is the same patience that the prophets of old demonstrated. I enjoy watching sports, though I do think that often sports in our day have taken a prominent place that they do not deserve in everyday life. That being said, often in a game, the score may get lopsided, and you will hear an announcer say they just have to get back to what they do best. Little by little, I have seen teams that seemed to be out of contention for the game crawl back into it by patiently just doing what they did best. The same is true for us—patience in the Christian life just consists of obeying the commandments of God, one after another until the plan of God is fulfilled and He takes all things and works them together for our good.

Likewise, we must seek to add patience through prayer. Romans 12:12 tells us, "Rejoicing in hope; patient in tribulation; continuing instant in prayer." Payer is how we log our complaints with God. Too often, we complain to everyone but the One who can actually do something about it. Read your Bible and you will find that the authors of Scripture complained to God about the circumstances that they were in. Complaining to God is okay, He knows what is in your heart anyway. He is not surprised that you are struggling, He expected it. It wouldn't be a trial if there was no hardship.

With trials come burdens, and God wants you to learn to pour out your complaint to Him instead of Facebook. The preface to Psalm 102 says, "A prayer of the afflicted when he is overwhelmed, and poureth out his complaint unto the Lord." That particular Scripture is the pouring out of a complaint, and that is what we are to do. When Hannah came to the temple in bitter prayer, she wept before the Lord. Eli approached her to find out what the problem was. "And Hannah answered and said, No, my lord, I *am* a woman of a sorrowful spirit: I have drunk neither wine nor strong drink, but have poured out my soul before theLORD. Count not thine handmaid for a daughter of Belial: for out of the abundance of my complaint and grief have I spoken hitherto" (1 Samuel 1:15–16). God heard and answered her prayer, and He wants to hear and answer yours as well.

Finally, we add patience by remembering that Christ will return. It says in James 5:8, "Be ye also patient; stablish your hearts: for the coming of the Lord draweth nigh." All the testing that we are facing will be over when we see Him. The thing that we must do is follow the example of Moses of whom the Bible says: "By faith he forsook Egypt, not fearing the wrath of the king: for he endured, as seeing him who is invisible" (Hebrews 11:27). Getting a good view of God now will help you have patience until His return. There is a joy and peace that is found in His presence now and a greater joy waiting in His presence to come.

By learning this practice of patience, we, like Joseph, can ultimately seize triumph from the tragedies that come in our lives. How are you doing in adding this grace into your life? Are you rebelling against it, or are you embracing the gift of trial with joy to obtain the promise of patience?

WHOSE FAULT IS IT THAT YOU'RE SAD?

> And it came to pass as they emptied their sacks, that, behold, every man's bundle of money *was* in his sack: and when *both* they and their father saw the bundles of money, they were afraid. And Jacob their father said unto them, Me have ye bereaved *of my children*: Joseph *is* not, and Simeon *is* not, and ye will take Benjamin *away*: all these things are against me. And Reuben spake unto his father, saying, Slay my two sons, if I bring him not to thee: deliver him into my hand, and I will bring him to thee again. And he said, My son shall not go down with you; for his brother is dead, and he is left alone: if mischief befall him by the way in the which ye go, then shall ye bring down my gray hairs with sorrow to the grave.
>
> Genesis 42:35–38

The life of Jacob paints an interesting picture. As a young man, he deceived his father because of his mother's counsel and was forced to flee his home because of his brother's anger. He met and fell in love with a beautiful young woman named Rachel for whom he labored fourteen years to marry. After another several years of service to his father-in-law, he departed somewhat with a conflict, accusing his father-in-law of unfair wages, and took his family back home. Along the way, God was dealing with him, and he was responding until the object of his affection—his wife—died. From the time that Rachel died until this point in the Scripture, you don't read at all about Jacob speaking to God or of God speaking to Jacob. Jacob sank down in unbiblical grief and began to blame everyone else around him for all of his troubles. If you look in these verses, you see him try to fix blame on his other children for the loss of his sons. The issue I want to examine here is not on who is to blame, but the issue of blame. I want to ask you, whose fault is it that you are sad? Jacob said, "All these things are against me. Everyone is against me, everyone is out to hurt me." He had his eyes fixed squarely upon every hurt that he had had.

Some people spend all of their time looking for someone to blame for their problems. I found one amusing article in a recent edition of *WORLD* magazine. The article chronicles the lawsuit of Timothy Dumouchel against Charter Communications, his Wisconsin cable company. He is threatening to sue Charter Communications because, he says, "the company has turned his entire family into lazy channel surfers against their will." He says he told them to discontinue the cable service, but they only stopped billing him. After repeated attempts to shut it down—as if he couldn't just turn it off—he now says the resulting TV addiction has harmed his family. I quote, "I believe the reason I smoke and drink every day and my wife eats too much is because we watched TV every day for the last four years." In other words, Charter made them addicted to TV. Now listen to this, Damouchel says he will "drop the suit in exchange for free lifetime internet service from Charter."

In *Discipleship Journal*, Don McCullough wrote: "John Killinger tells about the manager of a minor league baseball team who was so disgusted with his center fielder's performance that he ordered him to the dugout and assumed the position himself. The first ball that came into center field took a bad hop and hit the manager in the mouth. The next one was a high fly ball, which he lost in the glare of the sun—until it bounced off his forehead. The third was a hard line drive that he charged with outstretched arms; unfortunately, it flew between his hands and smacked his eye. Furious, he ran back to the dugout, grabbed the center fielder by the uniform, and shouted, 'You idiot! You've got center field so messed up that even I can't do a thing with it!'"

You see, it's not whether you win or lose, but where you place the blame. Let me say that as long as you are sitting in self-pity and looking for someone to blame, you will never get closure on any problem in your life. Blaming someone else does not give peace or rest; it only continues the cycle of endless pain. It has been said that people who are out to find fault seldom find anything else.

All blame is a waste of time. No matter how much fault you find in another, and regardless of how much you blame him, it will not change you. The only thing blame does is to keep the focus off you when you are looking for external reasons to explain your unhappiness or frustration. You may succeed in making another feel guilty of something by blaming them, but you won't succeed in changing whatever it is about you that is making you unhappy.

The problem that you have is not who is to blame but knowing what the real problem is. Often we misdiagnose what the problem is and then instead of being able to fix the problem, we spend all of our time being angry, burdened, or bitter over something that wasn't even an issue. The Devil is a master magician, he loves to pull the old sleight of hand on you and get you looking one way while he fools you the other; that is the issue with blame. Blame does not solve anything; it only compounds the problem.

The first time that we see the issue of blame in the Bible is with Adam and Eve in the garden.

> And when the woman saw that the tree *was* good for food, and that it *was* pleasant to the eyes, and a tree to be desired to make *one* wise, she took of the fruit thereof, and did eat, and gave also unto her husband with her; and he did eat. And the eyes of them both were opened, and they knew that they *were* naked; and they sewed fig leaves together, and made themselves aprons. And they heard the voice of the LORD God walking in the garden in the cool of the day: and Adam and his wife hid themselves from the presence of the LORD God amongst the trees of the garden. And the LORD God called unto Adam, and said unto him, Where *art* thou? And he said, I heard thy voice in the garden, and I was afraid, because I *was* naked; and I hid myself. And he said, Who told thee that thou *wast* naked? Hast thou eaten of the tree, whereof I commanded thee that thou shouldest not eat? And the man said, The woman whom thou gavest *to be* with me, she gave me of the tree, and I did eat. And the LORD God said unto the woman, What *is* this *that* thou hast done? And the woman said, The serpent beguiled me, and I did eat.
>
> Genesis 3:6–13

This is an interesting account because we see man's natural responses to sin. First, man wants to cover it with artificial coverings. We like to rename sin. We like to call it a disease because then we don't have power over it. We like to say we were born that way because then it is God's fault. We like to say that everyone is doing it because then there is no shame. We like to say that there is no God because then there is no accountability. We want to cover it, so we make up false religions to clothe ourselves with as a covering, we clothe ourselves with our works and our sacrifices, we cover ourselves with sanctimony and symbols of our own goodness. Yet, we cannot hide the fact that we are naked before God and everyone else. The king has no cloths on but is going around parading himself as if he does.

The second response to sin that we see here is that we hide. The guilt and shame of sin drive us to hide it. We don't want to be in the presence of God, or of those who know Him. When a person gets into sin and chooses to live in it, often they also choose to stop going to church because they don't want to hear that what they have chosen to do is wrong. And even if they don't hear about it, the conviction of being around the people of God, who are speaking of walking with Him and loving Him, is so great a dagger to their heart and conscience that they cannot stop thinking that everyone is judging them. They hide out so as not to be convicted and then begin to engage in the third response that we see here to sin.

The blame game: "It is my wife's fault, it is the Devil's fault, it is your fault, it is everyone's fault but mine. The preacher is too judgmental, he is always angry and yells at us." The truth is that if your preacher gets loud about sin, it is because he loves you too much to allow sin to ruin your life without a fight. But he is the recipient often of blame for someone's sinful choices or his wife or his children or the assistant pastors and their wives and children or some other person in the church, everyone else but the one actually committing the sin.

None of these solutions work; you cannot cover sin on your own, you cannot hide from sin, you cannot blame sin away. There is only one solution, only one way to get over the guilt of sin, and only one way to stop feeling sad. It begins with acknowledging that the problem is sin.

I don't know what the issue that your dealing with is. I don't know what the sadness that you're facing is, but I do know what the cause is. It is sin. It may not be your sin that stirred it up, but I can promise you that if you have fallen into blaming, anger, bitterness, resentment, and depression, it is your sin that is keeping you there. That is where Jacob was, he was unwilling to acknowledge that sin was the cause of death. The Bible says in Romans 6:23, "The wages of sin is death." There is no other source; everything else is just a method, not a cause. Cancer may be the tool that sin used, but the culprit is sin. Accidents, diseases, lunatics, war—it doesn't matter what the cause of death is; the blame is the same. It is not someone else's fault; the blame lies squarely at the feet of sin.

The problem is that we are all guilty. Romans 3:10–12 says: "As it is written, there is none righteous, no, not one: There is none that understandeth, there is none that seeketh after God. They are all gone out of the way, they are together become unprofitable; there is none that doeth good, no, not one."

Stop trying to justify your own sin and condemn another. Stop glossing over your own fault and pointing at those around you. If you are going to have any consolation regardless of the problem, the solution starts with taking personal responsibility for your own sin and accepting that sin is the problem. Don't tell me that you have never done wrong. Don't tell me that you are the one who is innocent of sin. There are none that can make that claim.

Jesus warned us in Matthew 7:1–5 about the danger of placing blame: "Judge not, that ye be not judged. For with what judgment ye judge, ye shall be judged: and with what measure ye mete, it shall be measured to you again. And why beholdest thou the mote that is in thy brother's eye, but considerest not the beam that is in thine own eye? Or how wilt thou say to thy brother, Let me pull out the mote out of thine eye; and, behold, a beam *is* in thine own eye? Thou hypocrite, first cast out the beam out of thine own eye; and then shalt thou see clearly to cast out the mote out of thy brother's eye."

Blaming someone else for having a splinter in their eye is useless when you still have a 2x4 in yours. How is it that we can always see someone else's problems and never our own? It is a statement that we cannot see the forest for the trees. Let me distinctly say today, if you are sad, if you are struggling with bitterness, if you are struggling with resentment or anger, the problem is not someone else; the problem is sin, and the source is your own heart.

The solution is confession, not of what they have done, but of how you have responded. Life is not about what happens to you, it is about how you respond to it. Multitudes have ruined their lives because of what someone else did and then blamed the other person, but you are the source of why your life has been what it is. You get to choose how you will respond. You get to choose to carry the offense or give it over to God. You get to choose whether to disable yourself with grief or false guilt or anger or bitterness. They may have done wrong, but your spirit is your choice. Your response is your choice.

No one will stand before God and say, "I would have done better but so and so wouldn't let me." You have a choice, you have a free will to decide with, and there is no one that is standing in your way but you. You can accept the blame or you can assign the blame but you cannot convince God of it. The only way to move past it is to confess that you have done wrong in spending your time blaming someone else and living in the bitterness, anger, and grief of the issue rather than in the peace of God.

Proverbs 28:13 tells us, "He that covereth his sins shall not prosper: but whoso confesseth and forsaketh *them* shall have mercy." There is no mercy, there is no forgiveness without confession and forsaking sin. It isn't just saying you are sorry; it is stopping the sin that is causing the problem. Often people are sorry that they got caught rather than that they have sinned. They are sorry that they feel cornered rather than that they have done wrong. That is why the Bible says to confess and forsake; the Bible also uses the word *repent*, meaning "to turn from." The great promise in the Bible is that when a person does confess and forsake, there is mercy and forgiveness.

1 John 1:9 reminds us, "If we confess our sins, he is faithful and just to forgive us *our* sins, and to cleanse us from all unrighteousness." The person looking for someone to blame will never know the peace of forgiveness. They will never know the grace and mercy of God, they will struggle in their condition, always pointing the finger of blame at someone else, and, in bitterness of soul and sorrow of spirit, will destroy their lives.

All the while, the rest that you seek is in Jesus. Jacob, for over twenty years, had no rest. For over twenty years, he had no fellowship with God because he had anchored his identity in other people who had failed him. Now others might have looked on Jacob and said that he was a man of faith. I am sure that, even at that time, he might have spoken of God. And I don't believe that he thought of forsaking God, although in practice, that is what he did. He had no recorded fellowship with God from the time that Rachel died until he saw Joseph again. He was stuck in the blame cycle and had no rest. His continual thought was that all these things were against him.

Maybe that is you today. You think that everything is against you, that you are constantly being put upon, that your life is one big struggle against everyone else. Let me say to you that you don't have to live that way. You cannot have peace as long as you keep pointing at others to blame and refuse to take responsibility for your responses. You cannot have rest without acknowledging that your situation is the result of your choices and confessing and forsaking the sin that has brought you to this point.

Jesus said in Matthew 11:28-30: "Come unto me, all *ye* that labour and are heavy laden, and I will give you rest. Take my yoke upon you, and learn of me; for I am meek and lowly in heart: and ye shall find rest unto your souls. For my yoke *is* easy, and my burden is light."

Do you have a burden that you have been carrying today? Do you have anger or bitterness that has been poisoning your life? Whose fault is it that you are sad? Will you accept that it is your fault? You can change it. You can come to Jesus and confess and forsake that sin that has kept you there, and you can take His yoke of humility upon you and allow Him to carry your burden. Then you will have rest for your soul. You will have peace and comfort of God.

HERE WE TEST AGAIN

And he commanded the steward of his house, saying, Fill the men's sacks *with* food, as much as they can carry, and put every man's money in his sack's mouth. And put my cup, the silver cup, in the sack's mouth of the youngest, and his corn money. And he did according to the word that Joseph had spoken. As soon as the morning was light, the men were sent away, they and their asses. *And* when they were gone out of the city, *and* not *yet* far off, Joseph said unto his steward, Up, follow after the men; and when thou dost overtake them, say unto them, Wherefore have ye rewarded evil for good? *Is* not this *it* in which my lord drinketh, and whereby indeed he divineth? ye have done evil in so doing. And he overtook them, and he spake unto them these same words. And they said unto him, Wherefore saith my lord these words? God forbid that thy servants should do according to this thing: Behold, the money, which we found in our sacks' mouths, we brought again unto thee out of the land of Canaan: how then should we steal out of thy lord's house silver or gold? With whomsoever of thy servants it be found, both let him die, and we also will be my lord's bondmen. And he said, Now also *let* it *be* according unto your words: he with whom it is found shall be my servant; and ye shall be blameless. Then they speedily took down every man his sack to the ground, and opened every man his sack. And he searched, *and* began at the eldest, and left at the youngest: and the cup was found in Benjamin's sack. Then they rent their clothes, and laded every man his ass, and returned to the city.

Genesis 44:1–13

Do you ever get the feeling that your life is an endless series of tests? That you are being proven once and again through trials? In our text, Joseph put his brothers through a final test. He had tested them concerning their honesty and humility—two things that he knew had been lacking in their life. He went on to test them concerning their loyalty toward his own brother Benjamin. Would they treat him the same way that they were treated? Would they forsake him and leave him for dead as well? Had there been any change in them at all?

The problem with the tests that God puts us through from a human perspective is that while we are going through them, we have no idea what they are about. We can see the intention of Joseph from this passage, but we can also see the desperation of his brothers as they were tested. When we consider the testing that we go through, we are often in the place of the brothers, with a sense of despair and confusion at the tests that we are going through.

Joe Scriven was a missionary from Ireland to Canada, working among the Iroquois Indians. He was joined by his fiancée who was also from Ireland. Just before the wedding, she was killed in an ice accident. Joe buried her with his own hands and a broken heart. A year later, in a letter to his mother, he reflected and wrote these words, "What a friend we have in Jesus, all our sins and griefs to bear! What a privilege to carry everything to God in prayer! Have we trials and temptations? Is there trouble anywhere? We should never be discouraged. Take it to the Lord in prayer."

I see, in this passage, a great and beautiful picture of what we as children of God are to do when we are tested. There are three things that I notice in this passage, which we should follow. Not surprisingly, the first thing that we see here is a show of humility. When this issue is brought forward, rather than justifying and blame-shifting, these men humbled themselves. We see this in a couple ways. First, they rent their clothes. This was a sign in the Old Testament of a broken heart, a completely humbled heart. They would take their shirt and rip it out to show that their heart was torn as well. It was a humbling experience for others to see your afflicted soul. The second thing that they did, which showed their humility, was bowing before Joseph when they got back to the house. Remember, Joseph was a picture of Christ here. When we are faced with a testing, we can respond with rebellion and get stiff-necked to our destruction, or we can humble ourselves and bow before God in seeking for His grace and mercy.

The natural man always wants to rise up against God. When we are tested, we tend to see other people or circumstances as the object at issue, and we get hardened against them. The truth is that we wrestle not against flesh and blood; we are not in opposition to one another. I am not your enemy and you are not my enemy. Our enemy is the Devil. The Devil, however, loves to pit us against one another. It is easy to get the view that this other person is the object of our problems and, thus, we give in to anger and bitterness. We can get bogged down in grief and self-pity, and when we do, our eyes and heart are blinded to the true enemy that is the Devil. Paul told the Corinthians in response to the issue of anger and forgiveness, "To whom ye forgive any thing, I *forgive* also: for if I forgave any thing, to whom I forgave *it*, for your sakes *forgave I it* in the person of Christ; Lest Satan should get an advantage of us: for we are not ignorant of his devices" (2 Corinthians 2:10–11).

The Devil loves to bind us in anger and unforgiveness and that can only happen as long as we allow our pride to keep us from humbling ourselves to God and one another. There is not an offense that God cannot cover; the Bible tells us that love covers a multitude of sins. In the trials that we face, we have the choice of anger at the people or circumstances, or humility to God. In the past, the brothers of Joseph had chosen the first, they had chosen anger when they had sold him into slavery. They had chosen bitterness when they cast him into the pit. Yet here we see that they had learned that these responses did them no spiritual good. They only cost them. Their anger and bitter response when they took things out on Joseph cost them a relationship with their father. Let me tell you this, you may think that you can contain the responses to trials to certain individuals, but you cannot. You don't know what other people it will spill over too if you yield to the flesh. You don't know what it might cost you in your relationship to God, you cannot judge that, and we are not ignorant of the Devil's devices. We do not have to blindly follow the desires and feelings of the flesh, but we can make the choice of humility to put it away. The wonderful thing about God is that His grace is sufficient to change our hearts. His grace is sufficient to change our feelings and our hurts, and bind us up if we are submitted to Him.

Consider what the Bible says about this issue of humility in James 4:6: "But he giveth more grace. Wherefore he saith, God resisteth the proud, but giveth grace unto the humble." Brethren, do you not know that for over twenty years, God had been resisting these men, their lives had been in hardship, and they had been in conflict because of their pride and lies. Yet, now when they come to this trial, by responding in humility rather than pride, they are going to find grace; their pride brought them to famine, but grace will bring them to provision. The difference between the two is pride and humility. You may say, "But I didn't cause this problem, this was not my fault." That may well be; however, God put you in it for a purpose. God orchestrated the situation. God moved the hearts of those involved to act both good and bad. You now have the choice to make of how you will respond to God in the situation. These men must have been quite perplexed. They had given their money for certain, but it was found in their sacks again. They had not taken anything that was not due them, and yet they are found with Joseph's cup. They could not understand why these things had happened. They could not grasp how things had developed the way that they did, but it was God who was working. Let me say that I have never yet gone through a trial and in the midst of it seen why things were working the way that they were. If that happened, I would not be in a trial. The hardest part of any trial is trusting God when I don't understand, forgiving when I don't feel like it, and sacrificing my desires for God's.

When we look at the Scriptures, we see that there are certain times in our lives where God prepares to take us through a testing. There are certain times where He brings us to the bank of the river and asks us to cross over, and then leads us to the cross and asks us to die to the flesh. Those are hard times; death is a painful process, but it is one that each of us must go through. I have been hurt in the ministry more times than I can count. I grew up in ministry. As a child, I was accused and blamed for things over and again. As a pastor, I have been the brunt of attacks and accusations and had church members as well as other preachers stab me in the back and try to hurt the church. There is not a pastor who wouldn't have to give the same testimony, and there is not a church member who wouldn't have to give the same testimony if they have been around very long. You know that there is one steadfast rule: People are jerks. Preachers are no exception, and neither are other church members. And I have sat alone and cried, when those whom I loved with all my heart hurt me, and I have, in my flesh, wanted to be angry and hateful and bitter. But I had to learn this (and all of us must): the only person I hurt, when I choose that, is myself and my family. They will go on and be free, and I will bind my heart in a prison and keep it there.

I cannot tell you how many times I have had to crawl up on the cross and kill this old sinful man and say I choose Jesus, I choose forgiveness, I choose God's love over my hate. The truth is that my feelings don't always respond immediately, but if I will obey the truth, they will follow eventually. I have made a decision a long time ago to humble myself. It may mean that others seem to get away with things that I feel are wrong. However, it is not up to me to execute vengeance in any way, that belongs to the Lord. My job is to exercise myself to humility and submit to what God wants to teach me and allow Him to have the glory in my life.

Here, Joseph's brothers finally learned that lesson, and it is not that it didn't hurt or that they understood; it is that they chose to humble themselves in spite of what they felt and how they wanted to respond, and God honored their humility.

The second thing that we see here is the result of humility that they took responsibility for the circumstances. You must, at some point, forget about who is to blame and just take the responsibility for where you are at. Now I didn't say that they took responsibility for something they didn't do, but they took responsibility for where they were. They couldn't change the circumstances, and so they said, "Listen, we will submit to be your servants. We will take the place of Benjamin. We will all be your servants, if you will just send him back to his father." Genesis 44:32–33 says, "For thy servant became surety for the lad unto my father, saying, If I bring him not unto thee, then I shall bear the blame to my father for ever. Now therefore, I pray thee, let thy servant abide instead of the lad a bondman to my lord; and let the lad go up with his brethren."

I tend to be very introspective at the end of a trial. I examine what happened and what I did. Where I was right and where I was wrong. You know what I have learned? I learned that there has never been a time in my life that I have done everything right. I hate that, it kills me to know that I have done things wrong, but I have. I wish that I didn't, but I am human and I mess up, even when I want to do right. Paul said in Romans 7:18-21: "For I know that in me (that is, in my flesh,) dwelleth no good thing: for to will is present with me; but *how* to perform that which is good I find not. For the good that I would I do not: but the evil which I would not, that I do. Now if I do that I would not, it is no more I that do it, but sin that dwelleth in me. I find then a law, that, when I would do good, evil is present with me."

I hate the flesh. I don't want it to get any traction in my life, but when I examine what I have done after a trial, I always find areas that the flesh got some dominance over. When that is the case, I have to take responsibility for them. I have to say I was wrong in this area. That doesn't mean everything was wrong, it doesn't mean that the total outcome was wrong; the grace of God often covers our errors in a miraculous way. But I don't want to deceive myself and think that I am always right. I want to grow! I want to be better for God. I want to be a better husband, I want to be a better father, I want to be a better pastor, and I want to be a better Christian. If I am going to be more for the Lord, I must examine what happened and what was right and what was wrong, and I must work to fix what was wrong in me. Over twenty years ago, I married my beautiful wife. I was a mess of a husband, but I determined to try not to make the same mistakes twice and I determined to try to learn from the problems that we faced and become a better husband. I am not the same man that she married over twenty years ago. I am not the same father I was when my first child was born. I am not the same pastor I was in 1994 when I started pastoring. It is not because I have just always done things right. It is because I determined, by the grace of God, I would not be arrogant about things that happen and I would examine myself to see where I had done wrong and I would seek by the Spirit of God to fix them. I have had to apologize to my wife for things, I have had to apologize to my children for things, I have apologized to churches for things. Apologizing is not a weakness; I am stronger now because of it.

I also have had to learn that taking responsibility for things done wrong can, if we are not careful, open the door to the accuser to begin to abuse that situation. I want you to know that when it is confessed to God, it is forgiven. When we give it over to Him, He covers it. John said in 1 John 3:20, "For if our heart condemn us, God is greater than our heart, and knoweth all things." When you apologize and turn things over to God, you have to be careful not to allow the Devil to abuse you through false guilt. You cannot spend the rest of your days trying to make it up to everyone else. You just determine not to do it again to the best of your ability. The old accuser of the brethren loves to abuse the saints. He loves to attack our hearts and condemn us, but greater is He who is within us than he who is within the world. We have been delivered from the kingdom of darkness and we have been translated into the kingdom of His dear Son. The Devil doesn't have the right to oppress the child of God and he must be reminded of it through claiming the blood of Jesus Christ.

Otherwise, you can allow false guilt to keep you bound in an unscriptural state of mind. Turn it over to God and let Him make you free! But, brethren, you cannot be free as long as you are in denial about what you did, and you cannot be made free as long as you refuse to examine yourself and take responsibility for where you are.

The third thing I see that they did here was they kept the commitments that they had made. They humbled themselves, took responsibility for where they were, and kept the commitments that they had made. They could have said, "Well, we didn't want this to happen, but, Benjamin you are on your own. We are out of here. You shouldn't have done that. Sorry. See you later." They determined they would not leave their brother behind; they would not go back on the commitment they had made to their father. The same should be true of us. We should not allow trials to cause us to forsake the commitments we have made to our heavenly Father. To turn back is to give victory to the Devil in our lives.

Faith is proven in the decision to walk forward for the Lord when everything in your flesh says sit down and quit. I have told you before, God does not judge you on how you feel; He will judge you on what you do. Everything in them may have said, "Forget it, leave him, and let's go. How could he have been so foolish to steal these things? How could he have done this to us?" But instead, they said, "We have made a commitment to our father and nothing will turn us back from him. Nothing will stop us from fulfilling that which we have promised to him." I want you to know that it doesn't matter if everyone else turns aside; you are still responsible to God for what you have committed. It doesn't matter if everyone else gives up; you can still press on. It doesn't matter if everyone else does wrong; you can do right. If everyone else forsakes God, you can fight on because on the side of the Lord there is strength and power. On the side of the Lord, there is comfort in trial and victory in faith. On the side of the Lord, there is healing for hurts and reward for faithfulness.

Yet, these things can only be obtained by doing things God's way. They can only be obtained by obedience to God's Word and yielding to the Holy Spirit of God rather than the yearning of our flesh and feelings. The trial is not to destroy you; it is to prove you, to purify you, to perfect you. It is your decision, though, what it actually does.

GOD BROUGHT ME HERE

Then Joseph could not refrain himself before all them that stood by him; and he cried, Cause every man to go out from me. And there stood no man with him, while Joseph made himself known unto his brethren. And he wept aloud: and the Egyptians and the house of Pharaoh heard. And Joseph said unto his brethren, I *am* Joseph; doth my father yet live? And his brethren could not answer him; for they were troubled at his presence. And Joseph said unto his brethren, Come near to me, I pray you. And they came near. And he said, I *am* Joseph your brother, whom ye sold into Egypt. Now therefore be not grieved, nor angry with yourselves, that ye sold me hither: for God did send me before you to preserve life. For these two years *hath* the famine *been* in the land: and yet *there are* five years, in the which *there shall* neither *be* earing nor harvest. And God sent me before you to preserve you a posterity in the earth, and to save your lives by a great deliverance. So now *it was* not you *that* sent me hither, but God: and he hath made me a father to Pharaoh, and lord of all his house, and a ruler throughout all the land of Egypt. Haste ye, and go up to my father, and say unto him, Thus saith thy son Joseph, God hath made me lord of all Egypt: come down unto me, tarry not: And thou shalt dwell in the land of Goshen, and thou shalt be near unto me, thou, and thy children, and thy children's children, and thy flocks, and thy herds, and all that thou hast: And there will I nourish thee; for yet *there are* five years of famine; lest thou, and thy household, and all that thou hast, come to poverty. And, behold, your eyes see, and the eyes of my brother Benjamin, that *it is* my mouth that speaketh unto you. And ye shall tell my father of all my glory in Egypt, and of all that ye have seen; and ye shall haste and bring down my father hither. And he fell upon his brother Benjamin's neck, and wept; and Benjamin wept upon his neck. Moreover he kissed all his brethren, and wept upon them: and after that his brethren talked with him.

Genesis 45:1–15

The testing is finally over, and the long chapter of Joseph's exile has come to an end. The truth has been revealed, and the family is reunited. This reunion is quite different from what you might have imagined. This isn't how it goes on daytime television; there are no accusations and fistfights, there is reconciliation and joy. Hard to believe that twenty years earlier, they abused Joseph, sold him into slavery, and forgot him for dead, and now he was saying, "Don't worry about it, God was working through you to bring me to this point so I could save you."

That goes so far from our flesh, that is so contrary to our thinking, yet that is exactly what God had done. Let's all admit right here at the onset of this, that Joseph was vastly more spiritual than virtually all of us. This is an unusual man, who had lived a life of trial and testing and had come forth from it with a right heart. This man was the epitome of what Job said in Job 23:10, "But he knoweth the way that I take: *when* he hath tried me, I shall come forth as gold." How did he do it? How did he come to the place where he could forgive such a dramatic betrayal and weep with joy at the opportunity not only to forgive but also to bless those who had hurt him? This truly is the key in our comprehension of getting victory in trials—it is the key to becoming better rather than bitter.

It can be summed up in one thought: God is in control. Listen to what he says in Genesis 45:5-8 again: "Now therefore be not grieved, nor angry with yourselves, that ye sold me hither: for God did send me before you to preserve life. For these two years *hath* the famine *been* in the land: and yet *there are* five years, in the which *there shall* neither *be* earing nor harvest. And God sent me before you to preserve you a posterity in the earth, and to save your lives by a great deliverance. So now *it was* not you *that* sent me hither, but God: and he hath made me a father to Pharaoh, and lord of all his house, and a ruler throughout all the land of Egypt."

This is a uniquely Christian ethic; to believe that wrongs done to you by others were orchestrated by God to accomplish the purpose of being able to bless those who had wronged you. It is the fragrance of the crushed rose. It is the very literal example of Jesus Christ, betrayed and abused, mocked, scourged, and killed, and yet then three days later He arose to offer love and forgiveness to the very men who had called out for His crucifixion. That He loves, forgives, and saves all those who have violated His holy law and mocked His righteous name, this is the basis of the Christian ethic, and yet it is so rare for Christians to exercise themselves to it. It is so rare to not allow the Devil to twist the reigns of the mind to allow pride to refuse to humble ourselves to the very principle that is responsible for our own salvation.

I want you to understand that God is in control when things are going wrong in your life. God is righteous and good, even when He allows others to be turned against us. You might ask, "What do you mean? Would God really allow others to be turned against me?" Well, He allowed Joseph's brothers to be turned against him, He allowed Job's wife to be turned against him to the point that she said, "Curse God and die." He allowed Paul and Barnabas to be turned against one another. Yes, God allows hearts to be turned, and even will turn them Himself, in order to test and prove to us and in order to accomplish His will.

Romans 9:15–24 says:

"For he saith to Moses, I will have mercy on whom I will have mercy, and I will have compassion on whom I will have compassion. So then *it is* not of him that willeth, nor of him that runneth, but of God that sheweth mercy. For the scripture saith unto Pharaoh, Even for this same purpose have I raised thee up, that I might shew my power in thee, and that my name might be declared throughout all the earth. Therefore hath he mercy on whom he will *have mercy*, and whom he will he hardeneth. Thou wilt say then unto me, Why doth he yet find fault? For who hath resisted his will? Nay but, O man, who art thou that repliest against God? Shall the thing formed say to him that formed *it*, Why hast thou made me thus? Hath not the potter power over the clay, of the same lump to make one vessel unto honour, and another unto dishonour? *What* if God, willing to shew *his* wrath, and to make his power known, endured with much longsuffering the vessels of wrath fitted to destruction: And that he might make known the riches of his glory on the vessels of mercy, which he had afore prepared unto glory, Even us, whom he hath called, not of the Jews only, but also of the Gentiles?"

God allowed the Egyptians after this time to be hardened against the Jews so that He could accomplish His will in them. He allowed the Jews to be hardened and blinded to the gospel to allow you to be brought into His grace. Do you not think that He can or will move the hearts of others against you to prove and test you? Do you not think that He has the right to do as He will? He is God! "Who art thou that repliest against God?" (Romans 9:20). You are the clay, you are the vessel, but you are not the potter or the master, you are the thing formed, and occasionally He must break us down so that He can make us into something more usable and beautiful. To do that, God will at times move the hearts of those close to us against us. Why? Because He is God and He knows what we need when we need it. We can be angry about it or we can yield to Him and follow His example and be blessed by it in the end.

Proverbs 21:1 tells us, "The king's heart *is* in the hand of the LORD, *as* the rivers of water: he turneth it whithersoever he will." If God turns the heart of kings, how would we consider that He doesn't turn the heart of every man? Or do we only want Him to turn hearts when it means making us happy? Are we only willing for God to be sovereign when it means working things out the way that we wanted them to work? Are we wiser than God? Are we smarter than Him? Shall God repent for what He chooses to do? Or at that point, do we stop believing that God is in control and start blaming men and assume that God could not have directed them otherwise?

In truth, God gives man a free will. I am not saying that God refuses the free will of man; however, the free will of man works within the sovereignty of God, not without it. Do you think that God is so weak then that He cannot work out the circumstances of life without the willingness of man? Is God so dependent upon us that He is held captive by us? No, God is able to do exceedingly and abundantly above all that we could ask or think. God is able to accomplish whatever He commands, and no man will or can stand in between God and His sovereign will.

In such a way, God directs the affairs of men to bring about that which He desires for His children, both what we see as good and what we see as bad, because He sees what we cannot. He knows the end desire, and without adversity, we will never be what He desires us to be. So at times, God moves the hearts of those closest to us against us to prove us, to see if we are like Christ yet, or if He still has more work to do; to see if we are able to allow Him to be God in our lives, or if we are still trying to run things and fix things ourselves. Let's be honest, Joseph passed the test, and we fail over and over again. I praise God that the Bible says, "For a just *man* falleth seven times, and riseth up again: but the wicked shall fall into mischief" (Proverbs 24:16). When I fail, I can rise up and try again. I don't have to stay in defeat; I can turn my heart and walk in His path.

God is in control when things go wrong! He is in control when people are moved against us as it was here with Joseph. He is also in control when adversity comes in other areas. When God took the children of Job, God was still in control. When all that he possessed was destroyed, God was in control. When his health was gone, God was in control. We want to say that God is in control when things are good, but, brethren, if you believe the Bible, God is in control when nothing's good. When your children die, when you lose it all, when you are on the deathbed with the worst disease, God is still in control. You want to praise Him when things are good, God wants to know if you can praise Him when nothing's good. Job said in Job 1:21, "And said, Naked came I out of my mother's womb, and naked shall I return thither: the LORD gave, and the LORD hath taken away; blessed be the name of the LORD."

The danger that we face on both sides of life is that when we are blessed, we forget God, and when we suffer, we blame God. He is trying to teach us to praise Him regardless of the issues. This is what we see in the life of Joseph. For twenty years, he suffered, was down trodden, and was falsely accused and abused, but still he kept his eyes on God. He kept his spirit right and said, "God is in control, God is working on something here, and though I cannot see what it is, I will trust Him." Then, because of his trust in God, he was elevated from the gutter to grander. He went from the pit to the palace and now the question will be, "You trusted God when things were bad. Will you still be faithful to Him when things are good? Will you still be like Him when everyone says you don't have to, when you feel that you have arrived?"

Can I say that God is in control when things are bad, and God is in control when things are good? It is unfortunate that so many people forsake God in the dark times of their life. They walk away when they need Him most and allow the flesh to have dominance over them. It is equally disappointing though how many people hold on through the trial and receive the blessings on the other side and then in times of blessing forget that they needed God and walk away from Him thinking that they have arrived. When they finally get to the palace they longed for, they forget that they need God.

God is sovereign, and He can lift you up when you are low and put you down when you are up; it is His right as God. When we are exalted by God and if we allow pride to enter our hearts, He must humble us because the Bible tells us that God resists the proud but gives grace to the humble. What a wonderful example of the understanding of God's sovereignty that Joseph presents to us because he was humble when he was in the trial, and he remained humble when he was blessed for his faithfulness.

In God's marvelous grace, He orchestrated the reunion of this family after tragedy, and the joy that was present was because they yielded themselves to God. They recognized that He is in control. They acknowledged that they didn't know everything and that God can move the hearts of men for and against us as He willed to accomplish His will. The question then is not whether God is sovereign over the hearts of men, but how we will respond not to man but to God. Again remember, Joseph didn't put the blame on his brothers, he put it on God. He said, "God is the one that has done this." How we respond is our choice.

The Bible gives an illustration of how someone else responded to trials in Psalm 109. David was a man who was tried in very difficult ways. You remember he was the champion of Israel, and Saul began to hate him, and even to hunt him to kill him. For three years, David ran and hid in caves and was oppressed. Later, his son rose up against him, and the people turned against him, and he had to flee the throne. He went into exile for a period of time. Were these things of God? Was it God's will that these things happen? The answer is *yes*. God allowed them, and even used them. God could have prevented them, but God chose not to. He chose to overcome them instead. So in Psalm 109, David writes about the trials and tells us how he feels that God had forsaken him and that he had done his best, but people had returned hatred for his love. He tells God what he wishes would happen to those who had done him wrong and, beginning in verse 21, how he feels weak and emotionally unstable. He felt that everyone was looking at him and knew all of the issues and that he was now a reproach to them all. Then in the last few verses, David gives us the answer for all these problems and how to overcome the trials in the right way.

In Psalm 109:27–31, he says: "That they may know that this *is* thy hand; *that* thou, LORD, hast done it. Let them curse, but bless thou:

when they arise, let them be ashamed; but let thy servant rejoice. Let mine adversaries be clothed with shame, and let them cover themselves with their own confusion, as with a mantle. I will greatly praise the LORD with my mouth; yea, I will praise him among the multitude. For he shall stand at the right hand of the poor, to save *him* from those that condemn his soul."

1. God has done it. I may not know why, but I know who! And I know this too: that He is God and whatever He does is righteous. When I acknowledge that God is in control, it takes the power away from men to hold me captive with fear and dread. I am not any longer bound by the issues that I feel that they have done to me, because it is not them, it is my God and I am answerable to Him and Him alone.
2. The second thing that David says is that he will not only accept that it was God who brought these things to pass, but beyond that, He would make the choice to praise God for the trial rather than wallow in the misery of it. With my mouth, I will praise Him. When I praise God for the trial, I take the power away from the Devil to accuse me of the issues. When he starts to accuse me, I just turn it into praise for God for He was willing to teach me and count me worthy of growing as His child.

The last thing the Devil wants is to drive me closer to God, so if I will do this, he will begin to leave me alone about it. David said, "Men had no power here, and the Devil has no power here. All power belongs to God, and I will give Him the honor in it." Joseph did the same thing, he didn't blame his brothers. He said God was in control. He didn't hold anger and bitterness toward them. Instead, he was about to become a blessing to them because he kept his eyes on God rather than on man.

What you do with trials in your life is up to you. God has provided a path to victory and blessing, but you must choose to take it. I didn't say it was easy, it is contrary to the flesh, it is contrary to the natural man's thoughts. But I will tell you this - there is no other path to peace, there is no other way to victory, and the blessings of doing things God's way is beyond our comprehension. Joseph found out just how much God can bless you when you keep Him on the throne and accept His will in your life, even when it seems bad.

HOW TO GET THE BLESSING AFTER THE TRIAL

And the fame thereof was heard in Pharaoh's house, saying, Joseph's brethren are come: and it pleased Pharaoh well, and his servants. And Pharaoh said unto Joseph, Say unto thy brethren, This do ye; lade your beasts, and go, get you unto the land of Canaan; And take your father and your households, and come unto me: and I will give you the good of the land of Egypt, and ye shall eat the fat of the land. Now thou art commanded, this do ye; take you wagons out of the land of Egypt for your little ones, and for your wives, and bring your father, and come. Also regard not your stuff; for the good of all the land of Egypt *is* yours. And the children of Israel did so: and Joseph gave them wagons, according to the commandment of Pharaoh, and gave them provision for the way. To all of them he gave each man changes of raiment; but to Benjamin he gave three hundred *pieces* of silver, and five changes of raiment. And to his father he sent after this *manner*; ten asses laden with the good things of Egypt, and ten she asses laden with corn and bread and meat for his father by the way. So he sent his brethren away, and they departed: and he said unto them, See that ye fall not out by the way.

Genesis 45:16–24

One of the most blessed phrases in the Bible is, "It came to pass." Though it may seem that a trial has lasted forever, there is a time when the trial will end, and that's after God has accomplished His will in and for us. When we endure trials and yield to God in them, the end of a trial always brings a blessing. James 1:12 says, "Blessed *is* the man that endureth temptation: for when he is tried, he shall receive the crown of life, which the Lord hath promised to them that love him." In our text, we see some principles of how to get the blessing after the trial.

The first thing that I want you to see is that God wants to give you the blessing when you have endured the trial. God is good, He is always good. Even when we are in the midst of hard trials, He is good. It is important to keep our eyes on the truth of God's goodness. David said, Psalm 27:13 *"I had fainted*, unless I had believed to see the goodness of the LORD in the land of the living."

There are a lot of people who endured trials and never received the blessing because they fainted at the end. They allowed the trial to overcome them, and they allowed anger and bitterness to be the end result of a trial rather than giving the burden over to God. God has never done anything to hurt you. He has never done anything to damage you. But you and I can sometimes forget that He is good and that He is working for our good. We allow the burden of the trials to become a weight that would destroy us rather than strengthen us. There are two opposing forces in a trial, however. There is God, who has allowed the trial to purify and refine you, to bring you to the place of blessing and joy, and there is the tempter, whom God has allowed to test you and His will. Remember Job, God allowed the test, but it was Satan that performed the testing. Now the Devil's will is not for your good, he wants your destruction. He wants you to allow the flesh to win and destroy your relationship with God. He wants bitterness and vengeance to take root in your heart and for you to turn away from God rather than to Him.

Remember, we are in a spiritual battle as believers and the enemy has a will for your life too. The enemy wants you to quit. The enemy wants you to die spiritually and stop loving God. He enemy wants you to blame God and turn on God and God's people to hinder the work of God. So you are caught between two opposing purposes when you endure a trial—the purpose of God, which is good, and the purpose of the Devil, which is evil. How will you fare? How will you overcome? How will you receive the blessing from God rather than the curse of the Devil?

We learn from verse 19 of our text that when the trial is over, leave the trial behind. There is a time to let the trial go. Get your family up and move out of it. We have spoken before about how tragedies have a tendency to be markers for our memories. We tend to allow them to be the standard of before and after in our thinking. However, if we are going to get the blessing, there comes a point at which the trial has to be left behind. Paul said in Philippians 3:13, "Brethren, I count not myself to have apprehended: but *this* one thing *I do*, forgetting those things which are behind, and reaching forth unto those things which are before, you have a choice about where you go from here." There is no doubt that the natural tendency is to memorialize troubles, to set up a marker so that we will always remember it, but the Biblical plan is to put it behind us and move forward.

Some time ago, my oldest son went through a hard trial in his life. As we sat and talked, I told him that he would have to give it to the Lord if he was going to have peace in his life. But he responded, "Dad, how do you do that?" I stood up and asked him to come with me to the street. On our side of the street were the telephone poles, and I took him to the one closest to us. I said, "Look down the street and you can see the poles as far as the horizon. Tell me, which one is the biggest?" He looked for a minute and said, "I think the one beside us is the biggest." I said, "Good, come with me." And we walked to the next pole. I said, "Now, look and tell me which one you think is the biggest now." He looked back at the previous pole and then at the one beside us and said, "I guess that this one looks biggest." I said, "I thought the one back there was the biggest" to which he replied, "It was when we were by it, but now this one looks bigger." And then I told him, "Son, that is how trials are. When you are beside them, they seem like the biggest thing to ever come along, and if you pitch your tent by them and sit down there, they will always be that way. But if you will trust God and get up and walk down the street, the trial that you thought was the biggest will get smaller and smaller in your view until you cannot even see it anymore. You may remember that it was there, but it won't have the same power that it once had in your life."

The longer that you are anchored in the past, the longer the Devil has dominance over you. The longer you hold on to the trial, the longer it is until you will receive the blessings of God in your life. For twenty years, Jacob sat in his sorrow and allowed the burden to be the dominating thing in his life, and then he was told to just get up and move on. That is easier said than done, but it is an absolute necessity if you are going to receive the blessings of God again in your life.

Verse 20 of our text teaches us that if you are going to get the blessing, don't carry any baggage with you. Don't regard the stuff that you had, God has some new stuff for you. There are some people who get up to move on but take a sack full of momentous with them to remind them of all the issues of their past. If you want to really have the blessings of God, bury your dead out of your sight. Often when I do marriage counseling with people who had previously been divorced, one of the big issues is that they have carried baggage from their previous failed relationship into the new one. All the hard feelings and insecurities come along with them and their emotional bag is already full so that they create a self-fulfilling prophecy about the new relationship, and it eventually fails. Statistically, 75 percent of second marriages end in divorce because of this.

Let me create an illustration. You get the trash bagged up after a large family meal and you have two arms full of garbage to carry out. As you are carrying it out someone comes by and tosses you a bag of cash. You have two options—either hold on to the trash or drop it and grab the cash. The problem that we have is that too often we are so attached to the garbage that we won't let it go to get something better. Those problems that you went through, they are the garbage; what God has in store for you is the cash. How much baggage you take with you from a trial will determine how much blessing you can receive when you move on. You can only carry so much, either good or bad. If your arms are full of the bad, you cannot pick up much of the good. At some point, if you want more good you have to lay down the bad.

Verse 21 of our text shows us that God will provide all you need to make the move. The question always is, how do I lay down the baggage and move on? The answer is *by faith*. Faith is not asking God to help you do something, faith is asking God to do it. It is going to Him and acknowledging that you cannot do it. It is admitting defeat in the flesh and humbling yourself to Him and saying "I am weak, but thou art strong." I cannot win, but He cannot fail. Jesus said in, Luke 20:17-18: "And he beheld them and said, 'What is this then that is written, The stone which the builders rejected, the same is become the head of the corner? Whosoever shall fall upon that stone shall be broken; but on whomsoever it shall fall, it will grind him to powder.'"

The question is will you be broken by falling on Jesus, or will He have to fall on you in judgment because of your unwillingness to move on from the trial? Moving on is only difficult as long as we allow the flesh to be the ruling party in our lives. When we put the flesh down and put God in His rightful place of Lord in our lives, He will do what the flesh could never do. He will move us from the burden to the blessing.

When He does, you must put off the clothes of your trial and put on the new rament God has provided us as we see in verse 22 of our text. Isaiah 61:3 says, "To appoint unto them that mourn in Zion, to give unto them beauty for ashes, the oil of joy for mourning, the garment of praise for the spirit of heaviness; that they might be called trees of righteousness, the planting of the LORD, that he might be glorified." Remember when the brothers of Joseph had heard that they had the cup, they rent their clothes, tore them, and they were now clothes of mourning, tattered garments that were unfit for the family of the king to wear. Likewise, the garments of our trials must be put away. The heaviness and sorrow of the trial must be put away and praise to God and joy in the Holy Ghost must be put on.

It is time to start praising God and looking at all His blessings in your life and give Him the glory for the great things He has done. Start a stroke file if you need to and write down three things in the morning, at noon, and in the evening that you can see to thank God for. It is so easy to get our eyes on the negative that we forget that God is good. It is so easy to keep our eyes on the problems and not allow the good things to come into our view, to not allow ourselves to see the blessings of God because we are so focused on the bad things in our lives. We become blinded and only see things through the lens of offense or burden. Everything we see, we interpret as bad because of that. At some point, we must put it off and put on the perspective of praise.

We must choose to see things from God's perspective. From God's perspective, things seem different. From His perspective, trials seem small and blessings are big; from ours, trials are huge and blessings are small. We must stop looking at things from the wrong perspective. We must put off the old rags of the trial and put on the new garments of praise in our life and begin to look at things from God's view.

Then we see in verse 24 that it is important not to let anything stop you from receiving the blessing. I remember in Bible college, we had a rule in the school that said no one could have facial hair, unless it was for medical reasons or they had had it for over eight years. There was a man who came to school during my third semester at college and he had a beard. Brother Hays called him into his office on the first day of school and also asked me to come in. I wasn't sure why at the time, but I went in. Brother Hays asked him, "How long have you had the beard?" The man said, "Seven years." Brother Hays said, "Well, the rules say you have had to have it for eight, so you will have to shave it if you want to go to school here." Then he added, "Now, do you believe it is God's will for you to be in school here?" And the man said, "Yes, I do." So Brother Hays said, "Then don't let anything stop you from doing God's will."

That was an important lesson for me. I was going through some rough trials at the time, we were in hard financial straits, and there were many things against us personally. But I knew one thing: it was God's will for us to be in school. We determined not to let anything stop us from doing God's will. Some people let things stop them from doing God's will. They allow the burdens and trials to stop them. They allow friends and family to stop them. They allow the cares of this life and the worries of tomorrow to stop them. They allow things to get in the way of doing God's will and then turn aside in the way. They stop following God because they have allowed something to stop them. If you know God's will, don't let anything stand in the way of doing God's will with joy. Don't allow the Devil to put a bolder in your path and prevent you from moving forward to where God has provided the blessings. Move that thing out of the road and move on. There are some things in our path that will grab our attention and hold it, and it is important sometimes to just cover it and move on. Don't let anything stop you from doing God's will in your life!

Finally, we see in verse 28, if you are going to receive the blessing after the trial, you must accept your restored relationship. Jacob could not believe that Joseph was alive. Now, he had a choice—he could sit there in denial and refuse to move on, or he could get up and go prove it was true. The Devil wants you to believe that you will never have any happiness again. He wants you to believe that God has forsaken you and you will be alone forever. He wants you to think that there is no point in going, and you might as well just stay where you are. But he is a liar. Just over there, Jesus is waiting. He has a blessing for you, he has provision for you; all you have to do is come to Him. When you are going through a trial, you feel as though you have been forsaken. You pray and think that God cannot hear you, and you cry and think that He doesn't care. You feel betrayed and alone, but, friend, listen to me today, Jesus didn't forsake you. He was just busy preparing a better place for you. At the end of the trial, He calls to you and says, "Come to me and receive the blessing. Come to the place that I have prepared for you." It is up to you to accept that He is alive and loves you. He never forsook you, He was busy all the time preparing for you. It doesn't matter how dark the night was; the day is at hand. It doesn't matter how long the storm was; the calm is finally here—just as the poet said, "The darker the night, the brighter the light." There is no way that Jacob could have understood the joy of the restored relationship until it happened. David prayed, "Restore unto me the joy of thy salvation; and uphold me *with thy* free spirit" (Psalm 51:12). That is exactly what God wants to do for you today. He wants you to receive the blessing and abide in His joy. The choice is yours whether you will or not.

DIFFERENT WAYS TO DEAL WITH TRIALS

And *there was* no bread in all the land; for the famine *was* very sore, so that the land of Egypt and *all* the land of Canaan fainted by reason of the famine. And Joseph gathered up all the money that was found in the land of Egypt, and in the land of Canaan, for the corn which they bought: and Joseph brought the money into Pharaoh's house. And when money failed in the land of Egypt, and in the land of Canaan, all the Egyptians came unto Joseph, and said, Give us bread: for why should we die in thy presence? for the money faileth. And Joseph said, Give your cattle; and I will give you for your cattle, if money fail. And they brought their cattle unto Joseph: and Joseph gave them bread *in exchange* for horses, and for the flocks, and for the cattle of the herds, and for the asses: and he fed them with bread for all their cattle for that year. When that year was ended, they came unto him the second year, and said unto him, We will not hide *it* from my lord, how that our money is spent; my lord also hath our herds of cattle; there is not ought left in the sight of my lord, but our bodies, and our lands: Wherefore shall we die before thine eyes, both we and our land? buy us and our land for bread, and we and our land will be servants unto Pharaoh: and give *us* seed, that we may live, and not die, that the land be not desolate. And Joseph bought all the land of Egypt for Pharaoh; for the Egyptians sold every man his field, because the famine prevailed over them: so the land became Pharaoh's. And as for the people, he removed them to cities from *one* end of the borders of Egypt even to the *other* end thereof. Only the land of the priests bought he not; for the priests had a portion *assigned them* of Pharaoh, and did eat their portion which Pharaoh gave them: wherefore they sold not their lands. Then Joseph said unto the people, Behold, I have bought you this day and your land for Pharaoh: lo, *here is* seed for you, and ye shall sow the land. And it shall come to pass in the increase, that ye shall give the fifth *part* unto Pharaoh, and four parts shall be your own, for seed of the field, and for your food, and for them of your households, and for food for your little ones. And they said, Thou hast saved our lives: let us find grace in the sight of my lord, and we will be Pharaoh's servants. And Joseph made it a law over the land of Egypt unto this day, *that* Pharaoh should have the fifth *part*; except the land of the priests only, *which* became not Pharaoh's. And Israel dwelt in the land of Egypt, in the country of Goshen; and they had possessions therein, and grew, and multiplied exceedingly. And Jacob lived in the land of Egypt seventeen years: so the whole age of Jacob was an hundred forty and seven years. And the time drew nigh that Israel must die: and he called his son Joseph, and said unto him, If now I have found grace in thy sight, put, I pray thee, thy hand under my thigh, and deal kindly and truly with me; bury me not, I pray thee, in Egypt: But I will lie with my fathers, and thou shalt carry me out of Egypt, and bury me in their buryingplace. And he said, I will do as thou hast said. And he said, Swear unto me. And he sware unto him. And Israel bowed himself upon the bed's head.

Genesis 47:13–31

There is a definite difference in the way that the heathen deal with a trial from the way that the children of God, who are right with Him, deal with a trial. I clarify those who are right with Him because when we are not right, we have a tendency to try and deal with trials in the same way as the heathen. We revert back to the same wicked thinking that we had before and then reap the reward of our error. In our text, today we see a large contrast between what happens when the world goes through a trial and when those who are right with God go through it. I want you to remember that they are going through the same trial and that there is no difference in the trial here. The only difference here is on who they put their trust in.

First, let's consider the way that the world deals with a trial. Here, the trial is obviously the famine that was over all the land. Now we have never been through such a trial in our lifetimes. We live in a land of plenty and abundance. Most of us have as much food in our pantries as some stores have on their shelves in third-world countries, so we have a hard time identifying with the trial that they were going through here. Yet the principles are the same, regardless of the trial.

The first thing that the world trusted in during this trial was their money. They had sold all that corn and grain to Pharaoh during the seven years of plenty, and I am sure that they thought during that time that they had really hit the jackpot. They were rich; it was a time of abundance, But the law of supply and demand was in effect. When the grain was flowing like water, it wasn't worth as much, and so they sold low, but when there was not enough grain to go around, it was worth a lot more, so they had to buy high. It is always like that with sin and the Devil. People always sell themselves low to sin and end up paying a much higher price for it later.

The money began to run out, and for a few months things seemed like they would be okay. As a matter of fact, it was probably a few years that the money lasted. Eventually, when you are trusting in money, you will find that it will run out. And when it finally did, the panic started to set in. They had never experienced that problem before, they were used to being able to count on the economy, and their money was the envy of the world. No one had the abundance that Egypt had at that time.

When the money failed, they began to make demands and said to Joseph, "Give us bread, the money had failed, so just give it to us anyway." Now that would never have worked because the people were used to being wasteful just like we are. There was no way that they would have moderated the amount of grain that they ate at that time if they were allowed free access to the storehouse. Joseph knew that and said, "Welfare doesn't work. If you want this to last for the full seven years that we are going to need it, then we will have to continue on in the fashion that we know works, and it is still going to cost you something."

What else of value do you have? The cattle were the next easiest thing to use to purchase the grain. Now you may wonder why they didn't just eat the cattle, since it's food; however, you must remember what the cattle eat. If you don't have refrigeration and you kill a cow, you would have to eat it all really quickly; if you don't kill it, you have to feed it. If you don't have grain to feed yourself and there is a famine so that there is very little grass for the cattle to eat, then what good are the cattle? They would have had very little use for such things. Last year when we were in drought, people were selling livestock like crazy. They couldn't afford to feed it and they couldn't find enough water for it. What had once been considered wealth and profitable quickly became a burden and a drain to the provision. Last year would have been a good time to buy cattle. The only problem is you would have had nothing to feed or water them with either.

So in verse 17 of our text, they brought all their horses and cattle and flocks and herds, and for that they received bread for a whole year. There is a difference in things of monetary value and things of intrinsic value. Their money was probably made of gold and silver; however, ours is made of junk mettle and paper. There is actually no value in our money at all other than what our government says it is worth. However, a cow or a horse is worth what the market says it is worth. It is worth what someone is willing to give for it. Cattle have intrinsic value; it is good for food and, thus, has more value than money.

The interesting thing here is that once the money had run out, they began to trade away things of real wealth. The Devil believes this however, "And Satan answered the LORD, and said, Skin for skin, yea, all that a man hath will he give for his life" (Job 2:4). What the Devil has seen of men is that they will give up everything that they have to live, so they had no problem giving up their cattle and horses here for the bread that they needed to sustain their lives. They had nowhere else to turn to; Pharaoh was the provider of their needs, the government was the source of bread and life, so they gave their money and sold all their cattle to keep their lives.

After they had given all their money and sold all their cattle, they had very little left to offer, so they said in verse 19, "Wherefore shall we die before thine eyes, both we and our land? buy us and our land for bread, and we and our land will be servants unto Pharaoh: and give us seed, that we may live, and not die, that the land be not desolate."

How quickly they came to the place that they were willing to sell their inheritance and their own bodies to survive. I want you to know that this world has no care for the inheritance that you have received from your fathers. They are interested in what they can get, so they will take it how ever they can get it. The people began one by one to sell their land to Pharaoh and then their own bodies into slavery. One by one the famine overtook them so that before long all the land and all the people belonged to Pharaoh. They were his to do what he wanted with. So he began to move them where he wanted them and demand of them what he would. They became hirelings for the prophet of the pharaoh. Verse 24 tells us they all served him for 80 percent of what they had received before. Now to this world, the thought that they could continue to have corn and live was acceptable.

They gave up on the idea of freedom, they were told where to live, what to do, how much they could keep and how much they had to give to their master. They became slaves to the system. That is exactly what happens because of sin. Let's make some spiritual application here for just a minute. Sin always costs you more than you thought you would pay. There is a high cost to living in this world and by this world's system.

It will take your money, your possessions, your lands, and your body before it is done. It is amazing how many people are lost to this world's system, and yet the rest of them continue to go on like there was no problem, as if it was only a personal problem for those who had fallen into the trap. Yet, in sinful deception, they believe that they will never fall themselves. And each step that you take makes it easier to take the next step.

Do you think, that at the beginning of the famine, anyone in Egypt would have been open to the idea of just giving everything to Pharaoh and becoming his slave for life and for the lives of their children after them? No! Yet, one by one they gave up to the point that they thought, "This is such a little step from where we are right now. What difference does it make?" The incremental nature of sin is what makes it so deceptive. There is never a point that sin stops. It keeps taking you until it has consumed all of you. Remember, the Devil knows that the lost man will give up everything in exchange for his life, and so he offers false choices. He offers what appears to be life in exchange for what is actually a perpetual servitude.

The choices that sin offers are lies. There is no peace in sin, there is no joy in sin, there is no freedom in sin; it is always the path to poverty and slavery. Sin always deceives and destroys. James 1:15 says, "Then when lust hath conceived, it bringeth forth sin: and sin, when it is finished, bringeth forth death." Sin brings death every time without exception. I am not talking about the sin that others commit; I am talking about your sin. I am not just talking about the sin of those who are socially outcast. We sit in our insulated houses and churches and look out and say, "Boy the preacher sure is right. The sin of drugs costs people more than they thought it would. Man, the sin of alcohol costs them so much and makes them a slave. The sin of gambling, prostitution, and lustfulness, and yet many who sit in the pew are toying with the same things saying all along that they will not be caught and will not have to pay the same price."

I want you to know that it isn't just those sins that cost you more than you wanted to pay. Listen to me today, the sin of lying has a higher cost than you want to pay. The sin of gossip has a higher cost than you want to pay. The sin of anger has a higher cost than you want to pay, and it will put you into bondage and cost you your life. How many people have lost all that they thought they had control of because they would not keep their lips and destroyed their testimony and their relationships through gossip and anger? How many parents died lonely and sorrowful because they destroyed their homes with anger?

Then we might say, "But it won't cost what other people's sin cost." Friend, you have believed a lie. All sin leads to servitude. All sin leads to death. There is not some sliding scale of payment that the Devil will extract. He is interested in your destruction and will not stop until it is accomplished. He doesn't care what lie you believe as long as you believe a lie. If it is the lie of drugs alcohol and fornication, he will take it. If it is the lie of gossip, anger, and self righteousness, he will take it. The cost is the same, the destruction is just as real; it just occurs in a different way. The person who is in the painful prison of addiction and its torments is no less tormented than the person who is in the prison of bitterness and depression and its torments; it is just a different cell. They are both slaves to their sin, they are both miserable, they are both lost to the system of sin and have very little hope to escape in their own power.

I am glad today that there is a power greater than us. I am glad today that there is a power that is great enough to free us from our sin, regardless of what shape it comes in. I am not talking about the higher power of AA, a power of your own making. Whatever power you can make is controlled by you. Whatever power you can make is not greater than you. But there is a power that is greater than you, and it is the power that created you. It is God the heavenly Father, who is the creator of all and the judge of all. It is the Father who, because of His great love for us, gave His only begotten Son to be the payment for our sin debt and purchase our freedom from the penalty of sin. It is through Jesus Christ that we have the forgiveness from our sin.

It is through confession and repentance that we can come to Him and be saved from the penalty of our sin. Confession that we are sinners and that He is the only one who can save, and repentance from trusting in our own goodness or works to save us and putting all our trust in Him. That is what repentance means—to turn from one to another.

This world will take it all. If they haven't already gotten it all, then it is just a matter of time. You won't escape this world alive. Sin will kill you. As a matter of fact, it already has. Jesus said in John 3:18, "He that believeth on him is not condemned: but he that believeth not is condemned already, because he hath not believed in the name of the only begotten Son of God." John said in 1 John 5:11–12, "And this is the record, that God hath given to us eternal life, and this life is in his Son. He that hath the Son hath life; and he that hath not the Son of God hath not life."

I want you to see what the alternative is today to the destruction of the world through trials. I want you to see what the alternative is today to the judgment of sin in this world and the high cost that it has. In verse 27 of the text, we see the people of God in the same land and the same famine; however, we don't see the same results. Look at Genesis 47:27, "And Israel dwelt in the land of Egypt, in the country of Goshen; and they had possessions therein, and grew, and multiplied exceedingly." The cost of the world was not paid by the people of God. They were in the world but were not of the world, and God had prepared a provision for them in advance. Remember, Genesis 47:12 says, "And Joseph nourished his father, and his brethren, and all his father's household, with bread, according to their families."

In the days of Elijah, there was a famine, and God told Elijah to go to the brook, for there He had made a provision for him. Over and over again, we see that God provides for His people. The widow, during a time of famine, had a barrel of meal and a cruse of oil that never ran dry. And I want you to know today that God knows how to provide for His children when the rest of the world is selling themselves into slavery.

You don't have to be a slave to the world if you are a child of God, but let me remind you that the old world is always calling. The flesh is always calling, even to the children of God, to give in to the old nature and respond to trials the same way that we used to. There was a place of peace and provision for the people of God, but the world had no such place. There is always the tendency to refuse the path of the Lord, even for His children, and suffer with the world rather than be blessed with the saints. I have seen so many people who had the testimony of being saved, and yet sold themselves into some form of slavery to sin. Not to their eternal death, praise the Lord their soul was secure if they were saved, but in this life they experienced the pain of sin rather than the victory of life. Peter warned us about this in 1 Peter 5:9, "Whom resist stedfast in the faith, knowing that the same afflictions are accomplished in your brethren that are in the world." And again in 2 Peter 2:19, "While they promise them liberty, they themselves are the servants of corruption: for of whom a man is overcome, of the same is he brought in bondage."

If you are saved today, you have the choice of living in the blessing and provision of God, or suffering the pain of sin. You can yield yourself to the sin that this world does, or you can confess and forsake it, giving it to God and allowing Him to make you free from it. John 8:36 says, "If the Son therefore shall make you free, ye shall be free indeed."

If you are not the child of God today, if you have never received Jesus Christ as your personal Saviour, then you have no choice until you do. You cannot escape the servitude and death of sin by your own power. You must call upon Jesus Christ to be your Saviour, to be free from the chains of sin and death.

THINGS YOU NEED TO KNOW TO MAKE IT THROUGH LIFE

And when Joseph's brethren saw that their father was dead, they said, Joseph will peradventure hate us, and will certainly requite us all the evil which we did unto him. And they sent a messenger unto Joseph, saying, Thy father did command before he died, saying, So shall ye say unto Joseph, Forgive, I pray thee now, the trespass of thy brethren, and their sin; for they did unto thee evil: and now, we pray thee, forgive the trespass of the servants of the God of thy father. And Joseph wept when they spake unto him. And his brethren also went and fell down before his face; and they said, Behold, we *be* thy servants. And Joseph said unto them, Fear not: for *am* I in the place of God? But as for you, ye thought evil against me; *but* God meant it unto good, to bring to pass, as *it is* this day, to save much people alive. Now therefore fear ye not: I will nourish you, and your little ones. And he comforted them, and spake kindly unto them.

Genesis 50:15–21

Some days, I want to quit. I don't know about you, but some days that is how I feel. I have been told to quit, I have had reasons to quit, and I have at times even justified the idea of quitting. When I was a boy, my dad had a family meeting. He took our dictionary and, in front of our family, cut the word *quit* out of our dictionary and said, "We don't believe in this word and we are not going to use it. It isn't allowed in our home any longer, and we won't recognize it as an option."

So since there is not another option, I have to just keep going on. I am sure that throughout his life, Joseph must have felt the same way at times. When he was thrown in the pit by his brothers, the idea of quitting probably crossed his mind. When he was sold as a slave, it may have entered his thinking. When he was falsely accused by Potiphar's wife and thrown into prison, there may have been the temptation to quit. Year after year, time after time as his life seemed to go downhill further and further, I just cannot imagine that the idea never crossed his mind. He was a great man but he was also human.

There were some things that just wouldn't let him give up, there was something that caused him to get up and go another day. As a matter of fact, the things that we see revealed in him, in this passage, give us a great insight into the way that he was able to endure through such a life of hardship and trial. I believe that as we consider this passage, there are four things that Joseph says that teach us what he had learned that brought him through life.

1. Accept that you are not God.

Now that may seem like a silly statement, but it is true. Joseph said, "Am I in the place of God? There are too many people who say they understand that but don't live like it. There are some things that belong only to God and that they continually take unto themselves. Here are three things that belong to God alone. Daniel 9:7 says, "O

Lord, righteousness *belongeth* unto thee, understand this, you cannot manufacture any righteousness." It also says in Isaiah 64:6, "But we are all as an unclean *thing*, and all our righteousnesses *are* as filthy rags; and we all do fade as a leaf; and our iniquities, like the wind, have taken us away." Every good thing that you can do is insufficient to produce righteousness in you. Yet, people get so filled up with their own goodness. We become self-righteous and think of ourselves as better than others. When you ask the average person if they will go to heaven, they will say things like, "I think I am a pretty good person." They begin to compare themselves to others and think that compared to their neighbor, they are better, therefore, they must be righteous. God says, however, in Romans 3:10, "As it is written, there is none righteous, no, not one." What you need is not your good works but righteousness that supersedes that of men. Jesus said in Matthew 5:20, "For I say unto you, That except your righteousness shall exceed *the righteousness* of the scribes and Pharisees, ye shall in no case enter into the kingdom of heaven." Hear me today, the scribes and pharisees get a bad name, but they were exceptionally good people from a worldly perspective. Yet, God says that all their good works and all their labor in religious things were not sufficient. The righteousness that it takes to get to heaven must exceed this. The righteousness that you and I need is that which is through Jesus Christ. In 1 John 2:1, it says, "My little children, these things write I unto you, that ye sin not. And if any man sin, we have an advocate with the Father, Jesus Christ the righteous." What you and I need is to be made righteous because you cannot make yourself righteous. It says in 2 Corinthians 5:21, "For he hath made him *to be* sin for us, who knew no sin; that we might be made the righteousness of God in him."

The Bible goes on to say that not only does righteousness belong to God but also "Salvation *belongeth* unto the LORD" (Psalm 3:8). Salvation is not by any means for you choose, it belongs to the Lord, and it is His to declare and give. It doesn't matter what men think about it, it doesn't matter how men want it to be, it is God's and His alone to determine. I have talked to many people who have said that they are going to get to heaven their own way, but there is no other way than through faith in the Lord Jesus Christ. It says in Acts 4:12, "Neither is there salvation in any other: for there is none other name under heaven given among men, whereby we must be saved." Salvation does not belong to men to determine their own way, it does not belong to a church to bestow on those they deem worthy, and it does not belong to society to crown its best. No, it belongs to the Lord, and He gives it to all those who call upon Jesus Christ for salvation. The Bible declares Romans 10:9-13: "That if thou shalt confess with thy mouth the Lord Jesus, and shalt believe in thine heart that God hath raised him from the dead, thou shalt be saved. For with the heart man believeth unto righteousness; and with the mouth confession is made unto salvation. For the scripture saith, Whosoever believeth on him shall not be ashamed. For there is no difference between the Jew and the Greek: for the same Lord over all is rich unto all that call upon him. For whosoever shall call upon the name of the Lord shall be saved."

The third thing that the Bible says belongs only to God is found in Hebrews 10:30, "For we know him that hath said, Vengeance *belongeth* unto me, I will recompense, saith the Lord. And again, The Lord shall judge his people." There are many who take it upon themselves to exact vengeance upon their enemies. They seek to revenge themselves rather than give their hurts over to God. This is actually the basis of what Joseph was saying, "Is it my place to exact vengeance upon you, that belongs to God?" It is not my place to take revenge. If you are going to make it through life, you must realize that you are not God and you cannot take unto yourself those things that belong to Him alone. You cannot spend your life seeking revenge upon those who have wronged you. If you do, you will destroy your own life in the process.

2. Realize people will do you wrong.

Joseph said in verse 20 of our text, "But as for you, ye thought evil against me." We must understand that the largest part of our problem is the wrong expectation that others will do right. When you have the false idea that others are going to do what is right, you are setting yourself up under a curse; you have put your trust in them, and they will fail you. It says in Jeremiah 17:5, "Thus saith the LORD; Cursed *be* the man that trusteth in man, and maketh flesh his arm, and whose heart departeth from the LORD." The only one that you can trust in is God, people will fail you. David said in Psalm 62:5-7: "My soul, wait thou only upon God; for my expectation *is* from him. He only *is* my rock and my salvation: *he is* my defence; I shall not be moved. In God *is* my salvation and my glory: the rock of my strength, *and* my refuge, *is* in God."

One of the biggest tools that the Devil uses is to get men to have wrong expectations of others, to believe that everyone has your best interest at heart or that they will look out for you and your protection. If anyone should have thought that it was Joseph, it was his very brothers that cast him into the pit and sold him into slavery. If you could trust anyone, you would think it would be your own flesh and blood, but putting your trust in people will never work. What I am saying may sound cynical to you—I know it did when I first heard it said. But it is what God says; our trust must be in Him alone. God has allowed all other things to be flawed and failing so that we would know that He alone is worthy of our trust. I like the sign I saw that said, "In God we trust, all others pay cash."

You cannot trust in men, regardless of their position. I was reading something this week and found it interesting for a couple reasons. It was an excerpt of the diary of John Wesley, and it reads:

> Sunday, AM, May 5—Preached in St. Anne's. Was asked not to come back anymore.
>
> Sunday, PM, May 5—Preached in St. John's. Deacons said, "Get out and stay out."
>
> Sunday, AM, May 12—Preached in St. Jude's. Can't go back there either.
>
> Sunday, AM, May 19—Preached in St. Somebody Else's. Deacons called special meeting and said I couldn't return.
>
> Sunday, PM, May 19—Preached on street. Kicked off street.
>
> Sunday, AM, May 26—Preached in meadow. Chased out of meadow as bull was turned loose during service.
>
> Sunday, AM, June 2—Preached out at the edge of town. Kicked off the highway.
>
> Sunday, PM, June 2—Afternoon, preached in a pasture. Ten thousand people came out to hear me.

People in the church rejected him, deacons kicked him out, the police chased him off, and the farmers turned animals loose on him. Here he was concerned for the souls of men, and there was no one whom he could trust in. But when it seemed that all hope was gone, there was God! Brethren, when no one else does right, God is still there. When men fail you, God is still there. When Joseph was in the pit, God was still there. When he was in the servants' quarters, God was still there. When he was in the prison, God was still there. When all the men around him failed him and there was no one to trust in, God was still there. If you don't realize that men will fail you, then you will get discouraged in your life and you will not make it.

3. God can turn the wrong of men to good.

Joseph said in verse 20 of our text, "But God meant it unto good." Paul said in Romans 8:28, "And we know that all things work together for good to them that love God, to them who are the called according to his purpose." There is no bad thing that has ever happened to men that God cannot turn to good. He takes the broken and destitute and makes them whole and flourishing. He takes the weak things of this world and uses them to confound the mighty. That is why your hope must be in the Lord instead of men. It may be bad right now, there may seem to be no hope, the world may be mocking and scorning you, but if you will hold on to the Lord, there is always hope in Him because He takes the wrongs of men and makes them into victories. The key most often is just being patient and persistent.

John Killinger retells this story from *Atlantic Monthly* about the days of the great western cattle rancher:

> A little burro sometimes would be harnessed to a wild steed. Bucking and raging, convulsing like drunken sailors, the two would be turned loose like Laurel and Hardy to proceed out onto the desert range. They could be seen disappearing over the

horizon, the great steed dragging that little burro along and throwing him about like a bag of cream puffs. They might be gone for days, but eventually they would come back. The little burro would be seen first, trotting back across the horizon, leading the submissive steed in tow. Somewhere out there on the rim of the world, that steed would become exhausted from trying to get rid of the burro, and in that moment, the burro would take mastery and become the leader. And that is the way it is with the kingdom and its heroes, isn't it? The battle is to the determined, not to the outraged; to the committed, not to those who are merely dramatic.

The story is about how Andrew Jackson's boyhood friends just couldn't understand how he became a famous general and then the president of the United States. They knew of other men who had greater talent but who never succeeded. One of Jackson's friends said, "Why, Jim Brown, who lived right down the pike from Jackson, was not only smarter but he could throw Andy three times out of four in a wrestling match. But look where Andy is now." Another friend responded, "How did there happen to be a fourth time? Didn't they usually say three times and out?" "Sure, they were supposed to, but not Andy. He would never admit he was beat—he would never stay *throwed*. Jim Brown would get tired, and on the fourth try, Andrew Jackson would throw him and be the winner."

"The thing that counts is not how many times you are *throwed*, but whether you are willing to stay *throwed*." We will face setbacks, we will have trials, but we must take courage and go forward in faith. Then, through the Holy Spirit's power, we can be the eventual victor over sin and the world. The battle is the Lord's, so there is no excuse for us to stay "throwed"! We must remember that God takes all things and turns them for good, but that process may not happen overnight. It may take time, or years, but if we just keep getting up and going on like Joseph, God will take all the bad and make it into good for His glory. Someone once said, "The next mile is the only one a person really has to make."

4. God has a purpose in everything that He allows.

He finishes in verse 20 by saying this: "To bring to pass, as *it is* this day, to save much people alive." The trials that God is allowing in your life today may be for the purpose of saving many tomorrow. Those who face the greatest obstacles often achieve the greatest feats. I have said to you before that God never chose to prevent pain, suffering, and trials; He chose to overcome them. God has a purpose in what He allows us to go through, but if we are not careful, we will become discouraged and angry, and then bitterness will overcome our hearts, and we will quit. We will fail to endure to see the purpose of God fulfilled in our lives.

Had Noah not had faith in the purpose of God, he would have perished in the flood along with the others. Had David not had faith in the purpose of God, he would have shrunk from the battles that God used to establish him. Had Moses not had faith in the purpose of God, he would have stayed on the back side of the desert. Had Paul not had faith in the purpose of God, he would have abandoned the preaching of the gospel after he was beaten and left for dead. Not everything that happens in life is good. God never said that all things would be good. He said he would take all things and work them together for good. He has a purpose for all that He allows, and it is so that we might, by these things, be able to accomplish greater things than we could without them. Could a Hebrew boy become the second in the kingdom of Egypt? Could he single-handedly save the world from famine? With men, this is impossible, but God said, "I can do it. I will take a willing servant and put him through what would cause others to quit. I will take him through the fire of adversity and mold him into just the right form so that when he comes out on the other side, I will be able to save my people by his hand. I will use him in a way that I cannot use others, but it will take his faith in my purpose in his life."

What caused Joseph to endure such hard things? He knew he was not God, he knew men would do him wrong, he knew God would take all the wrongs and make them right, and he had faith in the purpose of God for his life. Is this also true of you? Can you lay your claim with Joseph in these things as well, or will you quit before you ever get to the victory? Will you turn aside before God is able turn the bad things in your life into good?

www.ingramcontent.com/pod-product-compliance
Ingram Content Group UK Ltd.
Pitfield, Milton Keynes, MK11 3LW, UK
UKHW022215230426
12048UKWH00016BA/850